SWAP
LS Engines
INTO *Chevelles &*
GM A-Bodies

1964-1972

Jefferson Bryant

CarTech®

CarTech®

CarTech®, Inc.
838 Lake Street South
Forest Lake, MN 55025
Phone: 651-277-1200 or 800-551-4754
Fax: 651-277-1203
www.cartechbooks.com

Edit by Paul Johnson
Layout by Monica Seiberlich

ISBN 978-1-61325-306-9
Item No. SA383

Library of Congress Cataloging-in-Publication Data Available

Written, edited, and designed in the U.S.A.
Printed in China
10 9 8 7 6 5 4 3 2 1

Title Page:
GM's LS and new LT1 engine platforms share some of the same technology but have some important differences. For swap projects, many of the same procedures for swapping an LS apply to the new LT platform. Upgraded from the LS series, the LT-series engine uses the same basic architecture, but it also features significant new technology, such as direct injection.

Back Cover Photos

Top:
General Motors brought out the LT4 in 2015. This is a supercharged version found in the Corvette Z06. The biggest differences from the LT1 to LT4 are lower compression and slightly stronger pistons and rods to handle the additional boost.

Middle:
In an LS swap project, late-model transmissions are often longer and require a different mounting position; therefore, the shifter needs to be relocated and the transmission tunnel modified.

Bottom Left:
I recommend pre-wiring the pump and pre-installing the hose fittings because once the tank has been installed, you do not have much room to do this.

Bottom Right:
For most swap projects, adapter plates are required to mount the Chevy small-block motor mounts to the LS block. But bolting the adapters to the engine is pretty simple: four socket head bolts and you are done.

DISTRIBUTION BY:

Europe
PGUK
63 Hatton Garden
London EC1N 8LE, England
Phone: 020 7061 1980 • Fax: 020 7242 3725
www.pguk.co.uk

Australia
Renniks Publications Ltd.
3/37-39 Green Street
Banksmeadow, NSW 2109, Australia
Phone: 2 9695 7055 • Fax: 2 9695 7355
www.renniks.com

CONTENTS

Acknowledgments 4
Inroduction 5

**Chapter 1: Modern V-8 Masterpieces:
The LS- and LT-Series Engine** 6
Gen III: A Revolution in V-8 Performance 7
Gen IV: Improving the Legend 7
Gen V: The LT-Series 8
Engine Swap Projects 9
Performance Project: The "Take-Out" Procedure
for a Vortec 5.3-Liter Salvage Yard Engine 10

Chapter 2: Motor Mounts 13
Chevy Adapter Mounts for the A-Body 15
LS Frame Stands 16
Transmission Mounts 19
Performance Project: Choosing a Driveline 23

**Chapter 3: Oil Pans, Pan Modifications
and Aftermarket Offerings** 27
Stock Oil Pans 27
Gen V Oil Pans 29
Aftermarket Gen III/IV Oil Pans 30
Performance Project: Modifying a Crossmember
for Oil Pan Clearance 35

Chapter 4: Accessory Drives and Cooling Systems..41
LT Engine Series 42
Vehicle Fitment with Stock Accessory Drives 42
Aftermarket Drives 44
Cooling Systems 46
Performance Project: Adding Power Steering to a
2014-up LT-Series Engine 54

Chapter 5: Transmissions 60
Automatic Transmissions 60
Manual Transmissions 65
Performance Project: 3- to 4-Speed Floor Shifter
Conversion 66
Performance Project: Fitting an Early T56 to an LS
Engine 69
Clutch Basics 81

Chapter 6: Wiring Harnesses and Wiring 84
Take-Out Harnesses 85
Cam Sensor Locations 85
Connectors for 1997–1998 LS1 Engines 87
Relays for 1997–1998 LS1 Engines 88
Connectors for 1999–2002 LS1 Engines 88
Relays for 1999–2002 LS1 Engines 89
2009-up LS3 ECM Connector Pinouts.....................90
LS3 Factory ECM Pinouts 90
2014-up LT1 ECM Connector Pinouts.....................91
Aftermarket Harnesses 93
Performance Project: Drive-by-Wire to
Drive-by-Cable Conversion 99

**Chapter 7: Engine Management Systems,
Tuning Software and Controllers** 102
Aftermarket Tuning Packages 104
Aftermarket Engine Management 107
Performance Project: Installing an Aftermarket
Transmission Controller 110

Chapter 8: Fuel System 114
Fuel Pumps 114
Inline Fuel Pumps 117
Performance Project: Installing a Phantom
Pump System 122

Chapter 9: Exhaust System 129
Exhaust Manifolds 129
Headers 132
Catalytic Converters 133
Air Intake 134
Performance Project: Installing a Pypes
Exhaust System 135
Performance Project: How to Properly Dimple
Headers 141

Source Guide 143

ACKNOWLEDGMENTS

This book represents years of research, coordination with businesses at the forefront of LS swaps movement, and countless hours of shop time performing LS swaps. I have relied on many people to help compile information and present it in the user-friendly format you see in this book. It allows you to perform your own LS swap into GM A-Body cars as efficiently as possible while avoiding typical problem areas and pitfalls.

The following people were instrumental in accomplishing this goal: Gray Frederick, American Powertrain; Matt Graces, American Powertrain; Dr. Jamie Meyer, Chevrolet Performance; Colt Collins, Chevrolet Performance; Bill Nye, Chevrolet Performance; Chris Douglas, Comp Cams Group; Trent Goodwin, Comp Cams Group; Bill Tichenor, Holley Performance; Blane Burnett, Holley Performance; Jeff Abbott Jr., Painless Performance; Don Lindfors, Pertronix; Pat McElreath, Red Dirt Rodz; Chris Franklin, Red Dirt Rodz; Aeromotive Inc.; Dirty Dingo Motorsports; LS1tech.com; Summit Racing; ATS; AutoKraft; HP Tuners; G Force Performance; Dynotech Engineering; and Magnaflow.

INTRODUCTION

GM A-Body muscle cars (Chevelle, Buick GS, Pontiac GTO, and Oldsmobile Cutlass) are some of the most popular vehicles for an LS engine project. A wide range of aftermarket support provides nearly anything you could possibly need to complete a swap project. Sifting through all of this can be confusing. Although the typical carbureted Chevy small-block or Chevy big-block is a relatively "bolt-in" procedure, swapping an LS engine into an A-Body car requires thorough planning, many different parts, and significant work. But it pays off with easy start-up, consistent performance in any weather conditions, and horsepower from 400 on up.

With this book, you can sort through each component of an LS swap into any GM A-Body from 1964 through 1972. The main components of an LS swap are the motor/transmission mounts, oil pan, transmission, engine control module (ECM) and wiring, accessory drive, and fuel system. The two most common positions for LS mounts are stock and forward. The stock position places the transmission bellhousing flange in the same location as a stock Chevy small-block. This works for older GM transmissions without much issue, but modern transmissions are larger and hit the transmission tunnel. Moving the engine forward about 1½ inches allows most modern automatics to fit without tunnel mods and reduces how much the tunnel needs to be modified for late-model manual transmissions, such as the popular T56.

Oil pan clearance is another key factor when performing an LS engine swap. LS engines have a variety of oil pan designs that fit many different GM chassis platforms, but most of them do not work well in the A-Body frame. However, several oil pans fit the A-Body, and the aftermarket offers many more options for direct fit for the Chevelle and its brethren.

The transmission crossmembers used in these cars vary by year and model, mainly convertibles and non-convertibles. Most A-Body cars have open-channel frames, which use a tubular crossmember. The convertibles, El Camino, and high-performance A-Bodies use a boxed frame, which has a formed plate steel crossmember. The chassis for both vehicles has multiple positions to match various transmissions. In most cases, you can keep your stock crossmember and simply move it to a new position in the frame or replace it with an aftermarket crossmember.

A myriad of components, accessories, and controllers are available for swap projects. The ECM for LS and Vortec engines work well even in high-horsepower boosted applications, but these engines also require special software that is either very simplistic or extremely complex. Hence, this limits the average mechanic doing a swap project. Aftermarket controllers are typically easy to tune and often offer advanced tuning parameters without special software. A handheld programmer is sufficient for the most basic tuning, and therefore it's easy to tune the stock ECM. An abundance of aftermarket and a few stock accessories on the front of the engine are available for A-Body swaps.

The fuel system is another critical component of an LS swap because nearly all of them require return lines and electric pumps. You can use either an in-tank pump or an external electric pump, both have benefits and drawbacks.

You will find information on all of these topics and many more inside this book to help you wade through the world of Swapping LS-series engines Into GM A-Body cars.

MODERN V-8 MASTERPIECES: THE LS- AND LT-SERIES ENGINE

Development for the Gen III engine began in 1991 after the short-lived LT1/LT4 engine failed to meet GM's performance expectations. General Motors essentially started from square one to create the new Gen III V-8 engine, which shared very little with the original small-block Chevy LT1/LT4 platform that it replaced. A phenomenal high-performance engine, the Gen III LS1 showcased modern engine technology while retaining the traditional pushrod valvetrain. The engine first appeared as the flagship engine in the 1997 Corvette, generating a groundswell of enthusiast interest. A series of high-performance Gen III/Gen IV engines followed it.

Although many refer to these as "LS" engines, the official nomenclature is Gen III and Gen IV. These remarkable engines produced class-leading performance and fuel efficiency. Street rodders, muscle car enthusiasts, and even sports car aficionados recognized the potential of the potent, compact V-8s and sought Gen III/IV engines for swapping into a wide range of vehicles. The factory small-block engines pushed out 350 hp at the low end of the scale and reached more than 500 hp at the top end. It seemed the horsepower wars from the late 1960s were back again. In addition, Gen III/IV engines transformed Chevrolet Performance's marketplace and they released a full complement of high-performance parts for these powerhouse engines.

The desire to swap these engines into other vehicles is at an all-time high. Finding an LS engine for your project can be as simple as a stroll through the local salvage yard, a website visit, or a phone call to your local dealer. You can select a "take-out" engine from a damaged or totaled vehicle in a salvage yard, build an engine from component parts, or

An assembly technician installs components on each Gen III/IV powerplant. All Gen III/IV engines are distributorless, and all but one are fuel injected. If you are buying a used engine, you need all the wiring and electronics for almost every engine swap, unless you are going to use an aftermarket controller. (Photo Courtesy General Motors)

pick out a crate engine with a warranty from many different LS engine dealers and Chevy Performance. Many different models of these venerable engines are available from a variety of sources.

Gen III: A Revolution in V-8 Performance

All aluminum and cast-iron blocks built from 1997 through 2004 are basically the same. However, there are some minor differences within this time frame, including an important internal difference. The outside diameter (OD) of the camshaft bore was changed in 2004. Although the cam itself remained the same, the bearing OD changed, and required a different set of cam bearings.

General Motors utilized the Gen III platform for the full range of GM trucks. With two years of experience under its belt, General Motors replaced the aging Gen I 305 and 350 small-block truck engine platform with Gen III engines. The new truck and SUV powertrain was offered in three displacements: 4.8-,

5.3-, and 6.0-liter. These V-8 engines were installed in every GM truck and SUV from 1999 to 2007. The 4.8- and 5.3-liter engines have the same aluminum cylinder heads. The Vortec truck engines have proven to be a popular swap because of their abundant availability. You can pick up a Vortec Gen III for next to nothing.

Gen IV: Improving the Legend

In 2005, when the Gen IV platform began replacing the popular Gen III, the evolution in pushrod engine technology took another step forward. Based on Gen III architecture, these new engines took advantage of displacement-on-demand

(DOD) technology, which General Motors called Active Fuel Management (AFM). With AFM, the engine alternates firing of the pistons among all eight to as few as four pistons, saving fuel and reducing emissions. Although the technology has been offered on the Gen IV platform, this engine series was designed to accept Variable Valve Timing (VVT) and to accept three valves per cylinder.

But that did not mean the Gen III disappeared from production in 2005. The LS1 was still in production for the Holden VE and W models and the LS6-powered Cadillac CTS-V, while the Chevy Performance division continued to offer both engines. In fact, Gen III engine production continued

The scalloped holes at the top right side of the main webs on the block illustrate the crankcase breathing holes. This promotes proper ventilation for the air and oil vapor in the Gen III/IV engines. (Photo Courtesy General Motors)

Pumping out 505 hp, the LS7 was the first dry-sump LS engine, and it's a favorite for swap projects because you don't have the oil pan clearance issues that you have with a wet-sump engine. In addition, this fourth-gen engine is one of the most powerful naturally aspirated engines and is standard equipment in the Corvette Z06 and Camaro Z28. (Photo Courtesy General Motors)

Cadillac and Chevrolet needed an engine to turn the CTS-V and ZL1 Camaro into street demons, so General Motors came up with the LSA. The slightly smaller Eaton supercharger reduces the overall output to 556 hp compared to the LS9. The LSA is also available as a crate engine. (Photo Courtesy General Motors)

The LS9 is the ultimate LS powerplant, making 638 hp with the intercooled supercharger. When it was released, it was the most powerful production engine ever made by a U.S. manufacturer. It was installed in the ZR1 Corvette and the ZL1 Camaro. The 6.2-liter engine is available as a crate engine from GM Performance. (Photo Courtesy General Motors)

In 2014, General Motors introduced the LT1, the next evolution in small-block pushrod engine technology. Upgraded from the LS-series, the LT-series engines share some basic architecture, but are a completely new line of engines.

The biggest advancement in the LT series is direct injection. Similar to diesel fuel systems, the mechanical pump pressurizes the fuel to more than 2,000 psi and injects it directly into the combustion chamber, ensuring there is no issue with atomization and yielding absolute control over the engine's fuel use. (Photo Courtesy General Motors)

built. In 2005, the truck engine line changed to the Gen IV platform, adding six new Gen IV blocks. By 2008, the 6.0-liter L76 and the 6.2-liter LS3 joined the Gen IV line. With the popularity of the Gen III and Gen IV engines, General Motors developed specially for the aftermarket the LS364 carbureted Gen IV engine and the LSX bare block for retrofitting and swapping.

To further push the Gen IV performance envelope, General Motors stepped up its game with two new ultra-high-performance engines to stay on top of the late-model horsepower wars: the LSA and the LS9, both based on the LS3 block.

The LSA is a supercharged 6.2 liter that utilizes a 1.9-liter roots-type Eaton supercharger to build 556 brake hp (flywheel) and 551 ft-lbs of torque. The LSA is available in the 2009–up Cadillac CTS-V models as well as the 2012–up ZL1 Camaro.

The LS9 also measures 6.2 liters, but uses a 2.3-liter Eaton Roots blower to generate the 638 bhp and 604 ft-lbs of torque, making it the most powerful GM V-8 ever produced. Just like the LS7, the LS9 features a 10.75-quart dry-sump oiling system. The LS9 is used in the 2009–2013 Corvette ZR1.

Gen V: The LT-Series

In 2013, General Motors released the Gen V platform and adorned it with the LT-series designation. Although not to be confused with Gen II Chevy small-blocks, this engine series will eventually replace the LS-series engine in all platforms. The Gen V shares the look of the III/IV series, but is an all-new engine platform. The LT series' biggest advancement is the use of direct injection. With this

for new vehicles until 2005 when two all-new engine platforms were released: the Gen IV LS2 and LS4.

In 2006, the LS7, the ultimate Gen IV engine, was installed in the Corvette Z06 and made quite an impression in the high-performance community. This fire-breathing small-block produced 505 hp and earned the distinction as the most powerful naturally aspirated production small-block Chevy engine ever

General Motors wasn't going to stop there, as it brought out the LT4 in 2015. This is a supercharged version found in the Corvette Z06. The biggest differences from the LT1 to LT4 are lower compression and slightly stronger pistons and rods to handle the additional boost. (Photo Courtesy General Motors)

system, fuel is sprayed directly into the combustion chamber at high pressure (2,175 psi for the LT1), increasing fuel economy and overall performance through better fuel atomization. Direct injection also makes cylinder deactivation more efficient, further increasing fuel economy. The 2014 LT1 Corvette can achieve as much as 29 mpg. Other advancements include piston-oiling jets, active fuel management, and continuous VVT.

Chevrolet Performance has released two crate versions of the Gen V: a naturally aspirated 6.2-liter 460-hp LT1, which is the same engine installed in the base-model C7 Corvette, and the supercharged 6.2-liter 650-hp LT4, which comes in the Z06 version of the C7 Corvette. The LT1 for Camaros is rated at 455 hp.

6.2 LT1

Making 460 hp without a supercharger is not easy, and to do so while hitting 29 mpg is even harder, but the LT1 does exactly that. The 4.06-inch bore combined with the 3.62-inch stroke creates an 11.5:1 compression ratio, which makes efficient use of the fuel pumped through the direct-injection nozzles. A forged crank, hypereutectic pistons, and forged powdered-metal rods yield light weight and durability. The

heads are conventional aluminum castings that feature lightweight sodium-filled valves.

6.2 LT4

To increase the output of the LT1, General Motors dropped a supercharger onto the 6.2 block to make 650 hp. To make that work long term, changes were made to the rotating assembly. The crank is the same, but the rods were slightly redesigned to increase strength in key areas. The LT4's pistons are forged and the combustion chamber was opened up, decreasing the compression ratio to a boost-friendly 10.0:1. The rotocast heads are stronger and better at handling higher heat ranges than a typical cast head. The valves are solid titanium and the oiling system is a dry-sump design.

Starting in 2014, all GMC/Chevrolet trucks and full-size SUVs with V-8 gasoline engines come with Gen V engines. Currently three truck versions are available: 4.3 (LT-based V-6), 5.3 V-8, and 6.2 V-8. The V-6 is an LT-series engine, essentially a V-8 with two cylinders cut off. The V-8s are the most common for trucks and SUVs.

5.3-liter L83

This engine features a 3.78 bore with 3.62 stroke. These engines make

355 hp and 383 ft-lbs of torque with gas, while producing 376 hp and 416 ft-lbs of torque with E85.

6.2-liter L86

The L86 is a modified LT1, making 420 hp and 460 ft-lbs of torque. The LT1 and L86 are very similar, down to the compression ratio of 11.5:1.

Engine Swap Projects

The purpose of most engine swaps is to increase performance. In almost all cases LS engines meet performance goals. Because the Gen III/IV engine platform represents the largest growing segment of the performance automotive aftermarket, many options are available for increasing the performance of an LS-series engine. Simple bolt-on components include items such as larger throttle bodies or high-flow intakes; serious performance upgrades include items such as high-lift camshafts and large-port cylinder heads.

Although the factory equips its high-performance LS engines with superchargers, a turbocharger is the most effective big-boost upgrade you can install. Driven off exhaust rather than drive belts, a turbo provides "free" horsepower. A 5.3 Vortec engine with a single turbo can make more than 500 hp with no other mods (other than a tune).

With so many options to choose from, Gen III/IV engine swaps have become more and more popular. Once you know where to find the engine that best suits your needs, performing the swap is the next step. The rest of this book deals with how to do this and covers most of the details. Although every car and swap is different, several aspects are common to all.

Swapping an LS-series engine is not the most complicated automotive endeavor. An average swapping project is fairly easy if it is carefully conceived, researched, and planned. The Gen III/IV engine families have footprint similar to the original small-block Chevy. If a traditional small-block Chevy can be swapped into a vehicle, you can certainly install an LS engine, but some minor adjustments such as re-arranging the drive pulleys and other components may be required. The possibilities are truly endless when it comes to LS swaps.

Although most builders are familiar with carburetors and how they work, fuel injection systems, computers, and wiring harness hook-ups intimidate many swappers. Electronics are a critical component of any swap. In most cases, you must carefully modify wiring harnesses, plugs, and wiring, or purchase the correct aftermarket components for plugging in the particular engine to a specific car. Shops such as Painless Performance provide the products and support to help simplify the wiring harness. Tuning companies such as HP Tuners and EFI Live can reprogram the engine control module (ECM) to adapt it for a swap. In the end, you have a more efficient powerplant with the ability to tune it better and faster.

You can install a carburetor on an LS engine, such as an LS364, and eliminate a big chunk of the electronics. In addition, you can use an aftermarket carbureted intake designed for LS-series engines. LS engines with carburetors are just as powerful and still take advantage of the electronic spark distribution using the one-coil-per-cylinder design. You still need a spark controller, though, because these engines do not have a provision for a traditional distributor, but these control boxes are very easy to wire up.

One of the biggest benefits of the new Gen III/IV engines is their efficiency. They were designed to meet strict Corporate Average Fuel Economy (CAFE) standards for new vehicles. These engines manage to meet fuel economy ratings while making significant horsepower numbers. In the past it was not possible for a small-block Chevy to make 400 hp and get 20 mpg. With an LS engine, it is not only achievable, it's standard.

The 2013 Z06 Corvette has an LS7 that cranks out 505 hp and maintains 24 mpg highway and 15 mpg city for a combined 18-mpg average. A Gen I small-block Chevy cannot get close to those numbers. A stock Vortec 5.3-liter with an overdrive automatic can produce 350 hp and 20 mpg with a custom ECM tune.

These factors combined make the Gen III/IV engines the most popular swap since the original small-block Chevy hit dealers in 1955. With so many variations, there is sure to be a Gen III/IV engine to suit your application.

One of the most popular swaps is the 1964–1972 GM A-Body platform. This generation of vehicles covers every GM make (except Cadillac) and features the most popular muscle car models. These include the Buick Special, Skylark, Sportwagon, and GS. Chevrolet cars are the Chevelle, Concours Estate Wagon, Nomad, Malibu, and El Camino. Oldsmobile models include the F85, Cutlass, Cutlass Supreme, Vista Cruiser, and Cutlass 442. Fiercely independent Pontiac A-Body cars are the Tempest, Safari, LeMans, and GTO. The differences among models means different requirements for installing an LS or LT engine, most notably the frame stands for the motor mounts.

Performance Project: The "Take-Out" Procedure for a Vortec 5.3-Liter Salvage Yard Engine

Although some swappers purchase crate engines or salvage yard take-out engines, you can save a lot of money by finding a wrecked vehicle and yanking the engine yourself. GMC and Chevy trucks are the most abundant source for LS-series engines, but it's important to find one with less than 200,000 miles on the odometer. When properly maintained, an LS engine can make 300,000 miles before needing a rebuild. An LS engine with 150,000 or fewer miles usually has a lot of life left and does not require a rebuild.

For this project, I bought a still-drivable 2003 Chevy 1500 truck with rear-end damage. The engine and transmission ran well and it could have been repaired. However, it had a salvage title and was a bargain at $500, so I went ahead with the swap. I rolled the truck into the shop and began stripping it down by removing the fenders. Although removing the fenders isn't required, it makes accessing all the bolts much easier and the truck is slated for the scrap yard anyway. Within 10 minutes the fenders were off.

1 *Under the hood of this 2003 Chevy 1500 lies a dormant beast; well, a potent powerplant anyway. The 5.3 Vortec engine is the most commonly swapped LS engine. It is also the most abundant. Ripe for the picking.*

2 *First, I started removing the fenders and grille. Next, I disconnected the airbox and removed the shrouds.*

3 *I removed the fenders and hood to gain access to the engine without having to work around those parts. This is much easier. I disconnected the wiring and removed it from the engine. This included the computer, located on the driver-side inner fenderwell.*

4 *The hose can be removed or cut because it will not be reused. I did leave the A/C system intact, as those parts are good salvage parts and opening them to the atmosphere leads to damage.*

Next, I removed the core support. You can leave the radiator in the car until you are ready to pull it. Two body bushings on the frame connect the core support with through-bolts; remove them. The fenders are attached to the core support with a couple of bolts as well. This opens the front of the engine, making removal from the chassis easier.

A lot of hoses and wires attach to the engine. The coolant needs to be drained; you can do this last if you prefer as it usually makes a mess. The A/C components (compressor, hoses, and condenser) can remain in the truck. You can't use the stock A/C compressor in swaps, so there is no point in purging the gas from the system. Carefully remove each wire connector from the engine, cut any zipties or straps holding the harness to the engine or chassis (don't cut any wires!), and remove the harness. The hoses can be removed or simply cut because you need new hoses for your swap install. The ECM is located on the driver's side of the vehicle.

At this point, the engine should be unfettered. If you are removing the engine and transmission as one unit, unbolt the transmission from its mount, support it with a jack, and remove the transmission crossmember. Disconnect the transmission wiring harness, shifter, driveshaft, and cooling lines. Unbolt the engine from the motor mounts on the frame and attach an engine hoist. Lift the engine (with the transmission attached) and slide it out of the chassis.

If you are taking just the engine, you need to support the front of the transmission from the ground first. Then use a flywheel turner to spin the flexplate until you reach each torque converter bolt and remove them all. At this point, you can unbolt the bellhousing and remove the engine separate from the transmission.

Because this is a drive-by-wire (DBW) vehicle, I removed the pedal and throttle actuator control (TAC) module and installed them in the swap project car. The TAC module is located on the firewall next to the power brake booster. Don't forget these two items; you will need them if you plan to use the stock computer. If not, take them anyway, someone will want them.

With a little degreaser and elbow grease, your new LS engine will be ready for prime time in just a few minutes. Don't forget to save the secondary sensors such as the mass airflow (MAF) sensor from the air inlet tube.

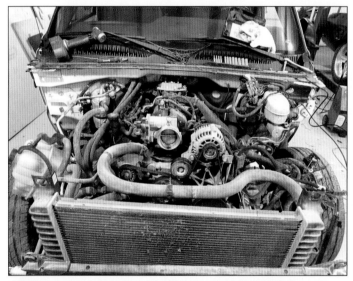

5 *The engine is now ready for removal; only the radiator stands in the way. I did this last to keep the mess to a minimum.*

6 *The TAC module is a key component of the drive-by-wire (DBW) system, so you need it and the wiring harness that goes with it.*

7 *The pedal mounts to the firewall. A few turns of the 10-mm bolts frees it from its humble cage and readies it for your A-Body ride.*

8 *With the engine on a stand, you can begin to prep it for your swap.*

MOTOR MOUNTS

The key to any swap is getting the engine into the chassis. This can be easy or it can take weeks to figure out, it all depends on the car. The 1968–1972 A-Body vehicles are easily converted to Chevy small-block frame mounts, but the earlier 1964–1967 A-Body cars are not as simple. General Motors certainly helped swappers by using the same motor mount design for all Gen III/IV engines, except the LS4, which is a front-wheel-drive platform. The LS-series engines share a footprint similar to the classic Chevy small-block engine's, so they fit in virtually any chassis that can house a Chevy small-block. That's a significant advantage to the swapper, as the conversion from a Chevy small-block to an LS can be as simple as adapter motor mounts.

The LS motor mount uses a four-bolt mount that bolts to the side of the engine block. This is not directly compatible with the standard three-bolt Chevy small-block mount. The most common solution for this change is converting the LS engine to the more usual early-style three-bolt engine mounts.

The original Chevy Gen I small-block from 1955 featured the three-bolt motor mount configuration, and the same motor mount pattern continued in production through the second-generation small-block, the LT1 and LT4. However, these engines are not to be confused with the new-generation 2014–up LT1 Gen V series. (Yes, General Motors reuses its nomenclature and it can be very confusing.)

Numerous companies make adapter plates to convert the LS mount to accept a Chevy small-block three-bolt mount. With so many adapters (hundreds of different brands are available), deciding which to use is the tough part.

When compared to the Chevy Gen I/II small-block, the stock LS engine motor mounts are located farther back toward the bellhousing. If a motor mount is bolted to the frame using these holes, in most vehicles the engine sits too far forward. This increases the nose weight of the car, causing instability.

Some adapter mounts are for specific applications, such as the Holley mounts for GM A-Body cars. In

Simple adapter plates are a common solution for many LS swaps' engine mounts. These plates from Hooker are made of billet aluminum. They bolt to the Gen III/IV four-bolt engine mount pad and allow a three-bolt GM motor mount to bolt on.

Bolting the adapters to the engine is simple: four socket head bolts and you are done. Make sure you use some anti-seize compound to prevent galling of the different metals.

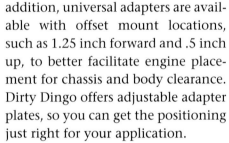

Not all adapters are the same. This kit from ATS flips the Chevy small-block mounts upside down to set the engine lower in the chassis. These are designed to fit the first-generation Camaro and the GM A-Body.

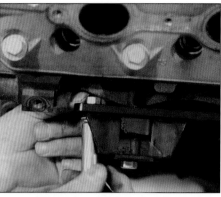

Some adapters, such as these Trans-Dapt mounts, require a lock nut on the back side of the plate. The external webbing makes it a bit of a pain to install the lock nuts, but these nuts are recommended to add extra security.

Once the locking nut is on the back-side, you tighten the bolt in the plate (which is also threaded) and then tighten the lock nut. If your adapter plates require nuts, you can use a box wrench with a tap on one side to hold the nut in place while you install it.

addition, universal adapters are available with offset mount locations, such as 1.25 inch forward and .5 inch up, to better facilitate engine placement for chassis and body clearance. Dirty Dingo offers adjustable adapter plates, so you can get the positioning just right for your application.

Simply bolting the adapter plate to the engine block provides mounting provisions for the old-style Chevy small-block three-bolt engine mount. This allows the LS-series engine to essentially drop right into the chassis without much effort.

For yet another alternative, American Touring Specialties (ATS) offers a set of LS adapter plates that feature an early-style motor mount in an upside-down configuration. ATS offers this arrangement so the engine can sit lower in the car and farther back toward the firewall, for better stability and a lower center of gravity. With these ATS mounts, an LS engine can be swapped into most any GM A-Body.

Depending on the motor mount, certain interference issues may occur, most commonly, oil pan to

crossmember and ground clearance, passenger-side valvecover to air conditioning compressor, and transmission bellhousing to transmission tunnel clearance.

Opinions vary as to which adapter style is the best fit for 1964–1972 A-Body platforms. The reality is that it depends on your engine, transmission, and component combination. This time frame in GM's history was the beginning of using corporate parts throughout the GM brands.

Before 1964, GM nameplates Cadillac, Chevy, Buick, and Oldsmobile manufactured and installed parts unique to their respective models; as a result, only a few components were shared across brands. In most cases, the chassis platform shared the frame or unibody structure, but very little else. In 1964 this changed, and suddenly GM brands were using "corporate" parts that interchanged between platforms, starting with suspension components and transmissions.

Engines, however, were still brand-specific. Although this does create a bit of a headache, the nice thing for 1968–1972 A-Body builders

is that all the frames are drilled for every engine stand. You can easily bolt a Chevelle engine stand into a Buick, Oldsmobile, or Pontiac frame.

Converting a 1968–1972 BOP (Buick, Olds, Pontiac) to work with the standard LS conversion mounts is handled one of two ways: convert to Chevy small-block frame stands or use LS-specific frame stands.

The early 1964–1967 A-Body cars are more difficult because these were not designed to accept all engine makes. A Buick used Buick mounts, a GTO/LeMans used Pontiac mounts, and so forth. A couple of aftermarket solutions do not require welding: Hooker (Holley) and BRP Hot Rods adapter mounts. They use existing holes in the frame to adapt the chassis to accept an LS engine mount. The Hooker mounts use the fourth-gen Camaro LS motor mounts, and the BRP mounts use a proprietary polyurethane mount. Conversion mounts that adapt non-Chevrolet A-Body frames to accept a Chevy small-block mount are readily available through companies such as Original Parts Group.

When adapter manufacturers talk

about "stock location," it is important to recognize that this refers to the original engine-to-transmission mating surface plane. LS engines are 1 inch shorter than a traditional Chevy small-block. Therefore, they do not have offset cylinders, and this means that the rear of the block is shorter than the Gen I block. Adapters that position an LS in the "stock location" place the transmission mating surface in the same location it would be if a Gen I Chevy small-block were installed in the vehicle.

Most LS engine adapters position the engine closer to the radiator, which is fine, because most of them do not run mechanical fans.

Chevy Adapter Mounts for the A-Body

Most adapter mounts are designed to work with the standard Chevy small-block three-bolt engine mount. For the A-Body, three different versions of motor mounts are offered: clamshell tall/narrow (early style), and short/wide.

Clamshell Mounts

The clamshell type is more common on later GM vehicles, but can

Tall/narrow, short/wide, and clamshell are the three main types of motor mount that have been used for the typical Chevy small-block frame stands. The clamshells are completely different from the other types. The tall/narrow mounts (left) are used for 350s and big-blocks. The short/wide mounts (right) are used on 307 cars. They both bolt to the engine, but wreak havoc on your engine position and install.

be found on 1964–1972s. These use a stamped steel pod that bolts to the engine with a steel and rubber mount that bolts to the frame. These can be used with most adapter mounts.

Tall/Narrow Mounts

These are the most common in Chevrolet A-Bodies. The tall/narrow distinction is confusing, however, as the frame pad is called short/narrow. Tall/narrow refers to the engine-mounted component. These Chevy small-block mounts from a small-block 350 were adapted to the big-block 396/454 engines in Chevrolet A-Body cars.

There is about a 1/4-inch difference in overall height between the tall/narrow (left) and the short/wide (right) versions, but it's not enough to allow some other components to fit. In addition, the narrow mounts don't sit down on wide 307 frame stands.

The center of the engine mounts measures $2\frac{3}{8}$ inches between the mounting ears and $2\frac{3}{26}$ inches from the center of the mounting bolt to the top of the engine mount pad. On the frame stand, the mounting pad measurements are $2\frac{3}{8}$ inches wide and $1\frac{5}{8}$ inches tall (crossmember to pad). The GM part numbers for these frame stands are 3980711 for left-hands, and 3980712 for right-hands.

These frame stands are readily available in the aftermarket as reproductions.

Short/Wide Mounts

Chevrolet used a different set of frame stands for the 307 than the 350 engine when installed in A-Body cars. The 307 frame stands are 1/2 inch taller than frame stands for the 350 engine. The width of the pad (where the two mounts come together) is also different. The 307 mounts are wider and measure $2\frac{5}{8}$ inches on both the frame stand and the engine block mount. However, the block mount measures $1\frac{3}{4}$ inch tall and therefore is shorter than the 350 version.

These are the most commonly sold mounts at the parts store, so it pays to know the difference.

The type of mount you need depends on your vehicle and the

Most A-Body cars have an interference issue with the inner tie-rod ends. The Mast oil pan for A-Body swaps has the best clearance, but you may need to raise the engine to get adequate clearance. The Hooker kit (shown) and similar kits have complementary parts that work as a complete system, and include mounts, pan, and headers.

Even with the right parts, some inner tie-rods are simply larger than others, which could result in light scrubbing, such as this on the bottom of the pan. This occurs at the extreme end of the turn radius.

Energy Suspension's correct tall/narrow mounts provide adequate clearance using the Trans-dapt adapters and Mast oil pan. The inner tie-rods just barely touch at full lock.

With the mounts on the block, the engine can be lowered into the car for a test fit. It is a good idea to test fit your engine before finalizing the details.

Hooker offers another LS swap solution for A-Body vehicles, particularly for non-Chevrolet brands that don't have factory Chevy small-block frame stands. Instead of searching for Chevy small-block stands, you can use these pieces along with a fourth-generation Camaro LS motor mount to place the engine in the correct position. These are available in both "stock" position and in the 2-inch-forward position.

accessory drive and oil pan you use. That being said, the best solution is to use the 350 version. These raise the engine a little higher than the 307, which provides better clearance for the oil pan and steering linkage. In most cases, you still need to raise the engine a little more to clear the steering linkage. About 1/2 inch usually works, depending on your oil pan and the angle of the engine/ transmission. Most adapter plates require the 350 version.

For the 1969 Chevelle project featured in this book, the 350 mounts were used with a set of Energy Suspension 31117G motor mounts and a Mast oil pan. The driver-side inner tie-rod cleared, but the passenger's side hit the pan. I raised the engine with an additional spacer block between the engine and the mount, which allowed everything to clear. The Energy Suspension mounts come with one spacer; I used two.

LS Frame Stands

Using an aftermarket stand is an alternative to sourcing original Chevy small-block frame stands. Several versions are available with the most

Under the hood of the 1971 Buick GS lies this 400-hp Buick 350. Although the engine is in great shape, it is time for something new. The latest generation of GM horsepower, the LT1, will do nicely.

Chevelle small-block 350 stands replaced the Buick stands and, indeed, it makes a difference. The Chevy 307 stands are different from the big-block stands. For the install, I bolted them in place using the forward holes in the frame. All 1968–1972 A-Body frames are drilled for all types of frame stands. I also used new Grade-8 bolts.

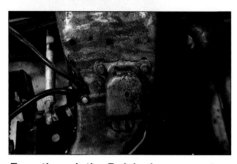

Even though the Buick shares most of the chassis components with the rest of the A-Body platform, the frame stands are not compatible. Only Chevy small-block mounts work for LS swap adapters, so the Chevy small-block mounts need to be installed. The Buick mounts shown here are set back way too far and too wide.

Accessing the bolts is tricky; you need a combination of wrenches and sockets to get to each of the nuts and bolts through access holes in the frame. The bolts pass through from the backside of the frame member.

common being the Hooker (Holley Performance) mounts. These fabricated steel mounts bolt to the 1968–1972 frames in the factory-drilled forward Chevy small-block position. The stands are designed to fit Gen-IV F-Body (1998–2002 Camaro) block mounts. The two versions of this mount are stock engine position and forward position.

Position A, or the forward position, is designed to reduce floorpan modifications for T56 6-speed transmissions and allows bolt-in installation of Turbo-Hydramatic 350, Turbo-Hydramatic 400, 2004R, 700R4, and 4L60/70 automatic transmissions. Position B, or stock engine position for a Gen I Chevy small-block, allows a TH350, TH400, or 2004R to mount to the engine using the stock crossmember without floor modifications. These mounts require extension floorpan mods with late-model transmissions and a custom transmission crossmember.

BRP offers a replacement mount that uses its proprietary Muscle Rods engine block mounts. This complete system includes a transmission crossmember and is designed to fit with Hedman Muscle Rod LS swap headers as well.

Earlier A-Body cars use a variety of adapters. Chevrolet models are easy, as Chevy small-block adapters are the standard. If you are swapping into a BOP A-Body car, you need to swap out the original mount for the Chevy small-block-type mounts. Although the non-Chevrolet mounts look as if they are the same or similar, they have different dimensions that are not compatible for completing a swap.

Another issue is that BOP frame stands are often in a different position than Chevrolet versions, similar to the later 1968–1972 frames. The most common solution is to use the 1964–1967 Chevelle 350 mounts for these early A-Body swaps.

Unlike the 1968–1972 models, the 1967-and-earlier frames use a single bolt pattern for all GM makes, three bolts in a triangular pattern. The frame stands themselves are different. This means that you must install Chevy small-block engine stands into the frame. Some swappers weld the engine stands to the frame, which demands a serious

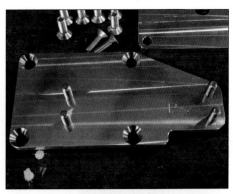

These Dirty Dingo mounts allow up to 2 inches of lateral movement. Adjustable motor mounts give you latitude to adjust the position of the engine and, therefore, flexibility to fit the exhaust, steering, air conditioning system, brake booster, and other underhood components. They are very popular because they offer more options for engine placement than other designs.

Adjustable motor mounts, with their many components, are more complicated to install, however. The slider (black piece) must be removed before the adapters are placed onto the block.

Here you can see the bare adapter. The "P" with an arrow dictates the side and front of the engine.

commitment to the placement of the engine. You must be 100-percent sure that the location is correct.

Fortunately, this is not necessary. The 1964–1967 Chevy small-block frame stands are readily available as reproductions.

Hooker frame stands provide an alternative to converting to the Chevy small-block mounts. The stock location in 1964–1967 cars presents a major component fitment problem similar to the issue in the later A-Body. Often there is not enough clearance between inner tie-rods and the oil pan, but also the transmission and A/C compressor fitment are an issue with the stock setback. Hooker 1964–1967 frame stands provide a viable solution because you can position the engine 1 inch forward from its stock location. When used in the complete Hooker LS swap system, all component clearance and fitment issues are alleviated.

BRP also makes kits for the 1964–1967 GM A-Body cars. Similar to kits for later vehicles, these bolt to the

A spacer plate comes with the adapters to locate the mounts for the proper height in the chassis. Leave these out and you will not be able to install the bolts into the frame stands.

If your block is aluminum, you need to use anti-seize on the supplied Grade-8 bolts to prevent the threads from galling.

The bolts have hex heads; be careful not to strip the hex head when torqueing the bolts.

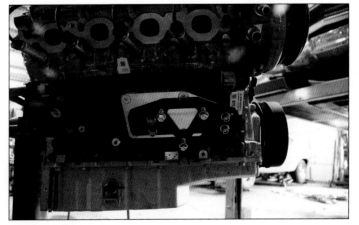

You mount sliding plates back onto the adapters using the installed studs. The final torqueing of the nuts and bolts is done after the position of the engine is set.

With the stands in place, set the new LT1 in the chassis, allowing you to check the fit for the oil pan and components.

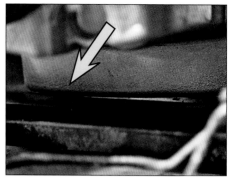

The LT1 wet-sump pan does not fit the stock chassis. The only option at the time was to modify the chassis. Right before press time, a new aftermarket oil pan was introduced by BRP Hot Rods; Dirty Dingo is developing one as well.

chassis and use either the Gen IV Camaro (Holley) or proprietary (BRP) motor mounts on the engine.

The 2014–up Gen V LT-series engines are similar to Gen III/IV blocks, but not enough to make them a simple drop-in replacement. At the current time, the aftermarket does not provide a full selection of motor mounts for the new generation of LT-series engines. There are a few options, however. The engine mounting location is the same, but the Gen V has a different bolt pattern. Dirty Dingo has sliding mounts for LT A-Body swaps that use the Chevy small-block frame stand and engine mount. The slider allows you to position the engine 2 inches forward, or aft, of its mounting position.

Transmission Mounts

Mounting an LS engine between the frame rails is only one part of the job; you also need to support the rear of the transmission. Although the LS bellhousing has an extra bolt at the top, its bellhousing pattern is the same as the Chevy small-block's.

This allows just about any traditional Chevy bolt-pattern bellhousing to bolt to an LS engine. Adapting the transmission mount to each vehicle is usually a combination of stock components modified with new mounts.

For most A-Body applications, the stock crossmember can be modified to fit late-model transmissions, including the T56 manual transmission and the 4L60E automatic. With the engine mounted to the frame, the transmission must be supported in front of the transmission mount

for access. The transmission bolts to the stock mount if it is properly aligned with the engine.

You need to consider firewall clearance when adapting an older GM transmission to an LS engine and installing it in an A-Body. The Gen I small-block was designed with offset cylinder heads that leave about 2 inches of space between the bell-housing mounting pad and the back of the cylinder heads. Consider this spacing issue when deciding whether to use the stock transmission.

Some late-model transmissions are larger than classic transmissions. They sometimes do not fit the transmission tunnel or do not fit in the stock location. But there are solutions for achieving enough clearance. The automatics have removable bellhousings and these often take up more room due to the bolt flanges. This is the reason sliding the engine forward 2 inches is a good idea. With the engine forward, most late-model 4-speed autos fit without any mods, as do T56 6-speed manuals.

The Hooker LS swap crossmember works for all transmission types and is very clean and lightweight. This unit was used in the Chevelle for the 5.3/Muncie swap shown in this book.

A-Body transmission crossmembers vary only by frame style. This tubular mount is used in most coupes, four-doors, and wagons. The crossmember has been hacked on and needs to be replaced, but it worked out for fitment in the 1969 Chevelle.

GM A-Body frames have multiple mounting points built in. All you might need to do is slide the factory crossmember into another set of holes. Remember, an early transmission sits about 2 inches farther back from the LS engine, depending on the engine mounts. The LS has a flush casting in the back, and unlike the Gen I Chevy small-block, there is no extra material on the back of the block. This convertible/performance chassis is boxed from the factory for strength. The crossmember bolts to the top of the chassis in contrast to the lower channel with open frames.

Gen III/IV engines do not have offset cylinder heads and, therefore, the cylinder heads are flush with back of the block. When it comes to planning your swap, you need to adjust for this lack of space between the bellhousing and the cylinder heads. The cylinder heads are not necessarily longer, but the back of the block is shorter. Adapter plates for the stock location provide a space of about 2 inches between the back of the engine and the stock transmission in the stock location. In turn, it's often necessary to relocate the transmission mount and/or move the transmission crossmember to bring the two components together, depending on the position of the motor mounts.

For stock-position adapter plates, the engine should match the same position for most GM automatic transmissions to fit in the stock location as well.

When choosing the transmission for your swap, carefully consider its location and how it will mount to the chassis. In the stock position, older GM transmissions such as Muncie 4-speeds, TH350/400s, and 2004Rs mount to their original location in the vehicle. For 1968–1972 cars, the stock crossmember fits and bolts into the correct location along the original nine-bolt pattern.

However, 1967-and-earlier cars have a four-bolt transmission cross-member pattern on the frame, limiting the options for the stock crossmember. Your engine position and transmission choice may require a modification to the factory crossmember or replacement with an aftermarket unit.

Another solution is the sliding transmission mount from G Force Performance. This special trans-mount bolts to the transmission and allows for up to 2 inches of travel fore and aft to reach the crossmember. These are particularly handy for swaps using sliding motor mounts; fewer mounting bolts means fewer options for mounting positions.

The late-model transmissions, including the manual Tremec T56 and GM 4L- and 6L-series automatics, are different. The T56 is a very long transmission, so fitting this into any A-Body with the stock setback requires fabricating a new transmission tunnel. The stock crossmember can be used in 1968–1972 A-Body cars with the stock setback adapters. Many owners, however, are not comfortable with or do not possess the skill set to fabricate a custom transmission tunnel. Cutting and welding in new sheet metal and chopping up the floorpan is a major undertaking, and many swappers are not interested in hacking up their car. The alternative is to use a forward-mount adapter with an aftermarket crossmember.

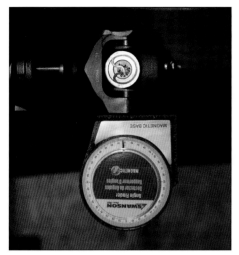

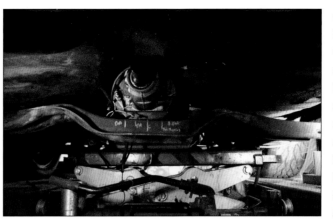

For an LT1 swap, the factory crossmember sits way too high, keeping the tailshaft from sitting at the correct angle. You could modify the crossmember or replace it with an aftermarket version. Lowering the factory crossmember requires dropping the center section because the exhaust doesn't clear if the entire unit is lowered. The transmission needs to drop about 3 inches.

The key to correct transmission angles is to position the tailshaft at an angle between 2 and 5 degrees, and it should match the rear pinion upward angle. Too little or too much causes vibrations and premature joint failure. An angle finder should be used to set the transmission at the proper angle. The U-joints must be "working" to last; if the joints are positioned at 0 degrees, they will burn up.

This allows the T56 to fit with minimal tunnel modifications.

For late-model automatics, you need to carefully consider the same factors. Here, the main issue is that they have bolt-on bellhousings, and that creates a clearance problem in the front of the transmission tunnel. The stock setback pushes the transmission back enough so that the bolt flange hits the tunnel. Serious modification is required to rectify the issue. Moving the engine forward 1 inch solves the problem, and the factory crossmember can be used as well.

When installing an LS engine, getting the driveline angle correct is critical in terms of strength and reliability. The transmission *must be* angled between 1 and 5 degrees downward on the yoke. For performance applications, 2 degrees is optimal. An angle finder (available at most hardware stores) can determine this angle. You place it against the tailshaft and let the needle rest until it points to the drive angle. If the stock crossmember bolts to the engine and the drive angle is between 1 and 5 degrees, it will work.

If the drive angle is not between 1 and 5 degrees, the crossmember must be modified so the driveshaft has an adequate angle. Several methods can solve this problem, but it depends on the crossmember you are using. Two versions of crossmembers for A-Body cars are available: a tubular unit for open-frame cars and a formed steel unit for boxed-frame cars (all convertibles, El Caminos, most GTOs and Stage 1 Buicks, and some Oldsmobiles).

With late-model transmissions, the most common issue is the tailshaft sitting too high in the car. Because the crossmember sits on top of the frame, it cannot be lowered easily. You can cut and weld the ends to lower the entire crossmember or you can drop the center; either one achieves the same end. The crossmember, however, also has raised sections for the exhaust, so lowering the center is the better option.

If that's not possible, a new crossmember is required. Numerous aftermarket crossmembers are available for open-channel frames. Some motor mount adapter brands, such as Hooker (Holley) and BRP Hot Rods, are complete systems, designed to work with the same brand's transmission crossmember. If you have a boxed frame, the open-frame transmission crossmembers don't work and you need a special crossmember. G Force Performance makes a heavy-duty crossmember that fits the A-Body boxed frame quite well and is perfect for LS swaps. BRP Hot Rods makes a boxed frame crossmember designed to work with its swap kit.

The keys here are driveline angles and keeping the tailshaft square between the frame rails. When fabricating crossmembers to support the transmission, use materials that are strong enough to hold the weight and torque of the transmission. Tubing (round or square) is a good material to use because it provides structural stability with less overall material thickness and weight. Flat-plate steel requires thicker material to achieve the same structural integrity. Angle steel is another excellent material for custom transmission crossmembers.

For the Buick, I opted for a G Force Performance Products crossmember because it's the only one available for boxed frames. To mount it, you drill out the stock bolt holes to 1/2 inch.

The G Force crossmember has a dropped-center mounting plate, so the transmission sits lower in the chassis for tunnel clearance, about 3 inches. You can always adjust the transmission mount with the provided mount spacers. I used one spacer on this install.

Placing the nuts into the chassis can be difficult; this trick helps you install them: Roll half a thread onto a long bolt and then thread the nuts onto the upper bolts. These nylock nuts are a little easier to work with than other nuts.

The beefy crossmember has large hoops for exhaust clearance and fits the chassis quite well. It's very strong and provides excellent support and strength, which helps maintain chassis strength. It is a little heavy.

I also installed the G Force sliding transmission mount so I had 2 inches of travel to mount the transmission to the crossmember. When sliding motor mounts have been installed, a sliding transmission gives you extra flexibility so you can correctly position the engine, transmission, and driveshaft for the best performance possible. A sliding transmission mount is especially helpful with sliding motor mounts because you can quickly exceed the reach of the factory slots in the crossmember.

I installed the mount and then slid the crossmember in place. You may need to remove the sliding section of the mount and roll the bolts into the crossmember slots because the bolts are actually studs and are made long for installs that need spacers.

Performance Project: Choosing a Driveline

When performing an engine swap, the driveshaft often needs to be replaced because it isn't compatible with powertrain and chassis requirements. Most often simply shortening the stock driveshaft is not a suitable solution. Your LS engine swap requires a significant investment that includes preparation, fabrication, time, money, and effort. Why use the same old driveshaft that will never work like a properly designed custom unit?

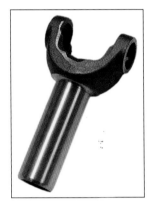

1 *This Dana cast slip yoke is strong enough and withstands up to about 800 hp, depending on the application. If it had been used, it would have saved the entire driveline. Unfortunately, the stock yoke broke, causing the shaft to become wadded up under the car. Once engine output approaches the 800-hp mark, you need to consider using a billet slip yoke because this is probably the strongest option available.*

In most cases, dropping in an LS engine increases the torque and horsepower output. Any time you increase the power output to the stock driveline, you must consider the impact on the stock driveshaft. Most factory driveshafts are balanced for a range of 3,000 to 3,500 rpm. Increasing shaft speed higher than 3,500 rpm can induce a parasitic effect. Steve Raymond of Dynotech Engineering said, "I have had several NASCAR teams tell us that our driveshaft saves them 3 to 7 hp on their chassis rolls dynamometers. That's why balance is important and why we manufacture shafts for about 85 to 90 percent of the NASCAR teams." The stock balance on the stock driveshaft is not good enough for anything but a stock engine.

Dynotech Engineering uses Balance Engineering's driveshaft balancers because they are considered the best in balance accuracy. Dynotech suggests balancing a performance driveshaft at a minimum of 5,000 rpm, and as high as 7,500 rpm. This ensures a properly tuned driveshaft that reduces parasitic loss.

Both slip and pinion yokes are critical driveline components that physically connect the transmission, driveshaft, and differential. Break one of these and you often experience expensive car damage and loss of control. That said, a cast yoke often

2 *The chances of breaking the pinion yoke are slight. The compact design places more material in important places, yielding a strong component. That is not to say a cast yoke is bulletproof, but a billet steel yoke such as this one from Mark Williams is pretty close. New yokes usually come with better joint caps, instead of lighter-weight stock-style U-bolts, which are prone to distorting the U-joint bearing caps.*

withstands up to 800 hp for most applications. But you can exceed 800 hp for certain cars such as lightweight hot rods with street tires because they put less strain on the driveline than a 4,000-pound Chevelle with slicks and 500 hp. You need to carefully consider this, however, and often it's better to upgrade.

Another option when using a cast pinion yoke is to use U-joint caps instead of the weaker stock-style U-bolt retainers. This increases the clamping force and eliminates the possibility of distorting the caps. New billet yokes typically come with the proper retaining caps.

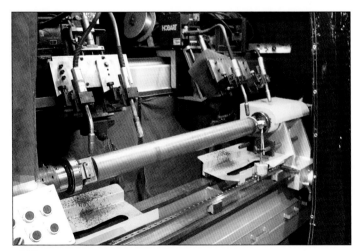

3 *Choosing your driveline shop is important. Dynotech Engineering uses CNC-operated welders to ensure a perfect weld every time.*

Along with balance, the length and diameter of the driveshaft directly affect the performance of the unit. Determining the required length for the driveshaft necessitates looking at several factors. The distance from the rear yoke to the transmission seal is the most important measurement because it determines the overall length of the driveshaft. Measure this length with the pinion yoke installed and the car at ride height. The pinion yoke influences the measurement, and changing from a cast-steel yoke to a billet pinion yoke can alter the length by as much as 3/4 inch.

Provide these measurements to the driveshaft shop and they can create the complete shaft with the required slip yoke and predetermined run-out for the slip yoke. For most applications, a run-out of 1 inch is more than enough to provide the play needed for suspension travel, so do not let a shop convince you to accept more run-out than that. Some transmission shops insist on running out 1-1/2 inches, but this could be disastrous and lead to driveshaft failure. With that much of the slip yoke hanging out of the transmission, there could be less than 3 inches of splined yoke in the transmission, thus creating a wobble in the yoke that would cause a heavy vibration at various RPM. Stick with the 1-inch rule.

Always measure the driveshaft length at drive height. If the vehicle is too low to crawl under it on the ground, jack up both ends and use jack stands under the rear end and front suspension; be careful to make sure all the stands are at the same height. The slightest variation in the suspension can throw off the measurement, resulting in a driveshaft that does not fit

6 This is a fully welded aluminum shaft and yoke. Note the clean, CNC-welded joint.

The function of "critical speed" (CS) factors into the length versus diameter rule. Critical speed is the RPM at which the driveshaft becomes unstable and begins to bend in the middle. This is also known as "jump roping." The longer and smaller (diameter) a driveshaft is, the slower its critical speed. Critical speed is felt as excessive vibration, and if run at CS too long, the unit will fail. To calculate the critical speed, you must know the length, diameter, wall thickness, and material module of elasticity. Then, using the critical speed calculation formula, you can plug in the numbers to calculate the driveshaft's critical speed.

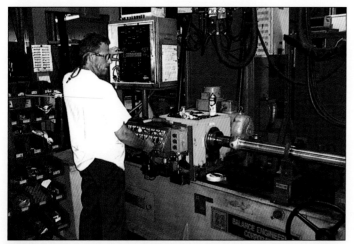

4 Once welded, the driveshaft must be balanced. This Balance Engineering balancer spins the shaft to 5,000 rpm, ensuring a proper balance for high-performance applications. This machine has the capability of revving to 7,500 rpm.

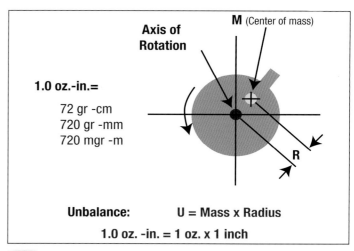

5 The formula for balancing the driveshaft is shown here. The red dot in the center is the actual rotational center and the yellow dot shows the center of mass. This represents an unbalanced shaft. The distance between the rotational center and the center mass determines the amount of weight needed to shift the center mass to the rotational mass.

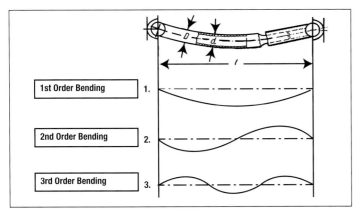

1st Order Bending	1.
2nd Order Bending	2.
3rd Order Bending	3.

7 *A driveshaft that is too small in diameter for its length can exhibit serious parasitic effects on the drivetrain. The first type of bend is referred to as first-order bending. Once this starts, the shaft often starts to flex up and down, and this is referred to as "jump roping." As a result the driver feels a significant vibration and the shaft and U-joints eventually fatigue.*

Driveshaft material is just as important as its length and diameter. Original equipment manufacturing (OEM) steel driveshafts are for just that, OEM power. An OEM shaft is rated for no more than 350 ft-lbs, or 350 to 400 hp. For high-performance use, drawn over mandrel (DOM) seamless tubing and chrome-moly steel are the two materials used. DOM steel is better than OEM steel, handling much more torque, up to 1,300 ft-lbs and 1,000 to 1,300 hp. DOM steel can be spun faster, as well, with its higher RPM rating, making it suitable for any stock LS application. This is a good choice for any car that does not need a lightweight unit.

The step up from a steel shaft is chrome-moly, which is the strongest material available. It's used in 3,000-hp Pro Stock cars. Chrome-moly steel tubing can be heat treated as well, raising the torsional strength 22 percent and increasing the critical speed 19 percent. Steel is heavy, which increases the load on the engine bandit so that it takes the engine longer to get to speed.

Reducing driveline weight is important, so lighter materials are sometimes a better choice. Aluminum is the most common performance driveshaft material. A lightweight aluminum shaft reduces rotational mass by freeing up horsepower from the engine and reducing parasitic loss. Aluminum driveshafts are strong but cannot hold as much torque as steel. Therefore, some custom driveshaft shops do not have "twist" guarantees on aluminum driveshafts. An aluminum driveshaft supports up to 900 ft-lbs, or 900 to 1,000 hp, making it a great lightweight choice for most muscle cars.

Carbon fiber, also an option, is the most efficient in terms of parasitic loss, but it is also the most expensive; it is not needed for high-performance street use, but often is used for high power figures, up to 1,200 ft-lbs, or 900 to 1,500 hp. Carbon-fiber driveshafts are strong and have a surprisingly high torsional strength, resisting twisting and reducing the shock factor on the rear end. Carbon fiber also has the highest critical speed module of elasticity, meaning the shaft doesn't flex at slower speeds, unlike other material components. Coupled with the highest critical speed factors and the light weight, a carbon-fiber driveshaft can free up as much as 5 hp over a stock steel driveshaft. When winning is everything, 5 hp might make the difference.

$$\left(\frac{923.44}{\substack{\text{Driveshaft} \\ \text{Length}}}\right)\sqrt{\left(\frac{\text{Module of Elasticity}}{(\text{Mat'l Density})(100)}\right)\left(10^8\right)\left(\left(\frac{\text{Tube Dia.}}{2}\right)^2 + \left(\frac{\text{Tube Dia.}}{2} - \frac{\text{Wall}}{\text{Thickness}}\right)^2\right)}$$

Attachment No.1 - Critical Speed Calculation

8 *Reaching critical speed causes first-order bending. This complex formula is used to calculate the critical speed for a driveshaft. All driveshafts have a critical speed depending on their length and diameter. The module of elasticity of the shaft material is an important part of the equation. Learning these numbers can be a little tricky because most shops keep the specific numbers close to the vest. For steel, the basic modulus of elasticity (MOE) is 30, aluminum is 10, and carbon fiber depends on the manufacturing processes used, so no numbers are available.*

9 *The type of U-joint used is more important than most people think. The "lubed for life" Spicer U-joint (left) is stronger than its same-sized greaseable counterpart (right).*

Once the driveshaft is measured and ready to build, there are a few other issues to consider. Phasing the U-joints with the weld-in yokes is an important part of the equation. With every rotation of a U-joint at any degree other than zero, a fourth-order vibration is generated. This shows up as a torsional pulse, which is felt as a significant vibration. By phasing the weld-in yokes to minimize the combined degrees of rotation, the fourth-order vibration is drastically reduced. The weld-in yokes need to be installed on the same plane; they can't be rotated off axis of one another.

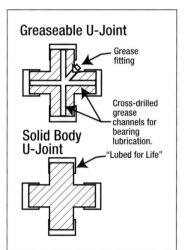

10 *This diagram shows the difference between the two types of joints. The greaseable joint (top) has less material in the center of the joint, reducing its strength and, therefore, torque level. A solid U-joint (bottom) does not require maintenance and is much stronger.*

it can be done, using crossover U-joints is not suggested as a long-term solution. The smaller size basically becomes a fuse and breaks eventually.

The type of joint, solid-body versus greaseable, is important as well. The Spicer-style solid-body U-joints come "lubed for life," and do not have grease zerk fittings. This makes them a little stronger because they do not have the stress risers created by the opening for the zerk fitting in a greaseable U-joint.

Building the right driveshaft for the application is critical; every high-performance vehicle should have a driveshaft professionally built by a shop that specializes in high-performance drivelines. Have your facts straight if you are going to have a local shop build your driveshaft. The shop or builder needs to stand behind its driveshaft 100 percent. Tell the shop it is for a high-performance application, which is very different from a stock driveshaft and needs to be held to a higher standard.

Ordering a driveshaft over the Internet from a reputable high-performance builder requires accurate measurements and clear instructions of what you have and what you need. In the end, you will receive a driveline that will be perfect for your swap.

The quality of U-joints makes a difference, and not just the brand, so you need to consider the design of the U-joint as well as the load capacity. The typical choice for most cars is 1310-series U-joints; for performance applications, however, the rugged 1350-series joints are the better choice. The larger the series number, the larger the trunnion.

Trunnions are the protruding shafts that the caps ride over. Larger trunnions equate to more torsional strength. Torsional forces are exerted in a twisting motion. Changing to a larger series U-joint is not a simple task; you can't just buy bigger joints. All yokes (slip, bolt-on, and weld-in) must match the desired joint size. You can opt for crossover U-joints, but they tend to not be as strong and they don't last as long. This allows you to mate a larger (or smaller) U-joint to the yoke.

For example, you buy a new driveshaft that comes with 1350 weld-in yokes, but your car has 1310 yokes for the transmission and rear differential. A 1350-to-1310 joint has a 1350 on one side and a 1310 on the other, allowing you to install the driveshaft until you replace the slip and bolt-on yokes. Although

11 *From left to right, 1350, 1330, and 1310 are the three most common sizes of U-joints. The 1310, the most common U-joint, is found in most cars. Performance yokes are made of the 1350 series U-joint, though larger and smaller units can be found. Make sure you use the same-series joint throughout the entire driveline. A drivetrain is only as strong as its weakest link.*

OIL PANS, PAN MODIFICATIONS AND AFTERMARKET OFFERINGS

Once you have selected compatible motor mounts for your project, the next step is to find the oil pan that fits your engine combination and A-Body car. Many stock oil pans are available for LS engines, each one having been designed for a specific chassis. With so many different oil pan options, there is confusion as to which oil pans fit which chassis.

The front crossmember and the engine mounts determine how the engine fits in the chassis and the oil pan clearance in relation to other suspension, steering, and chassis components. Each brand of engine mount is different, and the engine-mount towers used on the frames can differ by application as

well. Although several stock pans fit certain vehicles, they don't always fit as is, and there are different depths and clearances. Some motor mount adapters are designed to work only with certain pans; others are more universal.

Stock Oil Pans

Using a stock oil pan can greatly simplify your installation, provided you have the right one. Many stock oil pan designs are available, but only a few are desirable for engine swaps. The most commonly used stock oil pans are the 1998–2002 Camaro, the 2002–2006 truck, the C5 Corvette "Y" pan (also referred to

as the "batwing" because of the dual kickouts on the sides), LH8 or Hummer, and the CTS-V. These pans have proven to be the most versatile stock oil pans that fit many vehicles without modifications.

For GM A-Body cars, the list is shorter. Oil pan issues must be addressed when mocking up the motor mounts and modifying the front crossmember. Sump depth also needs to be considered, as several stock pans may clear the chassis, but the sump depth can become an issue when the sump hangs below the crossmember, especially on lowered vehicles.

In a typical installation, you may find that more than one pan fits your A-Body. Case in point: The LH8 oil pan (a special pan for the 5.3-powered Hummer H3) easily fits the wide range of 1964–1972 GM A-Body cars. However, with a typical adapter plate and motor mount installed, the LH8 pan rear sump hangs about 1½ inches below the engine crossmember, so standard suspension–height cars should have enough clearance on public roads. However, if the car

Oil pan selection is critical to proper engine fitment in the A-body chassis. Some stock pans fit, and there are plenty of aftermarket options too. This Holley Pan works great in all years of A-body chassis.

has a low ride height, especially on air-ride suspension, there may not be enough clearance between the pan and the pavement.

The BRP Muscle Rods motor mount kits use the LH8 oil pan, but the special motor mounts position the engine differently in the car than most other adapter kit installations. As such the LH8 pan provides enough clearance to avoid common road obstacles.

Each oil pan requires its own specific windage tray, pick-up tube, and dipstick. When purchasing an oil pan, make sure you purchase these parts with it, so you don't have to buy them later. Several blocks and oil pan configurations place the dipstick tube in the pan rather than in the block. If you have one of these engines and need to use a non-dipstick tube pan, the machined boss on the passenger's side of the block must be drilled out. Using a 3/8-inch drill bit, drill it through (about 1/8 inch of material), and then the tube slides right in.

F-Body Camaro/Firebird

The Camaro/Firebird oil pan (PN 12558762) was used on 1998–2002 Camaro/Firebird Gen III engines. But this pan *does not* fit 1964–1972 A-Body cars without modification because it interferes with the front crossmember, keeping the engine from sitting down on the mounts. About 2 inches of depth must be removed from the front edge of the rear sump, along with a large section of the front of the sump.

These oil pans are made of thick aluminum, and a welder with experience and the proper technique is required to correctly weld them. The aluminum oil pan must be TIG welded, and even an experienced welder can quickly ruin it. There-fore, unless you're an accomplished welder, you should consider buying a professionally modified or custom aftermarket oil pan.

It is possible to use the Camaro pan in 1964–1972 A-Body cars without modification. It depends on your engine/transmission package and chassis as to whether this pan fits unmodified.

Forward-placement mounts may result in crossmember interference. The F-Body oil pan's rear sump measures 5 inches deep, 11½ inches long, and 9½ inches wide. Most of the interference is at the shallow front section; the front-most section is flat for 4¼ inches and then slopes downward at a steep angle for 4¾ inches.

2002–2006 C/K Truck/Escalade

This oil pan (PN 12579273) is fitted to all 4.8-, 5.3-, and 6.0-liter C/K trucks and Escalades. It features a long, shallow front section (12¼ inches) with a crossmember-friendly, short, 8¾-inch-long rear sump. The rear sump is quite deep, though (8¼ inches), precluding it as a good candidate for most car applications. This pan can be used in the GM A-Body cars (Chevelle, GTO, Buick GS, etc.), but has a tendency to fall victim to road debris due to the deep sump. You can get away with this pan if you make a skid plate to protect the pan from debris. Your best bet is a different pan.

2007–up GM Truck

This oil pan (PN 12609074) is found on 2007-and-newer GM trucks with the 4.8-, 5.3-, 6.0-, and 6.2-liter Gen IV engines. Like the 2002–2006 C/K truck pan, the later pan has a shorter, shallow front section at 11½ inches and a slightly longer, rear sump at 9¾ inches. The rear sump depth remains the same at 8¼ inches.

Like the earlier truck pans, these have a deep rear sump that tends to hang down past the crossmember in 1964–1972 A-Bodies. Modifying them is a budget alternative to purchasing a new pan.

C5 Corvette "Y"

With one kickout on each side, this oil pan (PN 12561828) is typically referred to as the "batwing" pan because the kickouts resemble wings. This race-inspired design allows for consistent pickup coverage under high lateral G-force turns. The pan is very shallow (4¾ inches from top to bottom), and it has 20½-inch-wide kickouts that preclude it from working in most stock-chassis A-Body vehicles.

2004–2007, 2009–up Cadillac CTS-V

Available on the Cadillac CTS-V, this oil pan is essentially a hybrid of the F-Body and the C/K truck pans. The rear sump is 5½ inches deep, which is 3 inches less than the truck version and 1/2 inch deeper than the F-Body version. The shallow front section is 11 inches long, but this is shorter than the truck pan, yet longer than the F-Body. You can use standard adapter plates that set the motor low in the car, while clearing the engine crossmember. The CTS-V pan does hang below the front crossmember by about 1 inch on a 1964–1972 GM A-Body. It depends on which motor mounts are used, as some mounts such as the Trans Dapt adapter plates place the engine slightly higher in the car, reducing the amount of overhang. The later-model CTS-V cars with the LSA use a similar oil pan, with a few minor differences. The external dimensions are the same; however, the LSA pan has larger oil filter threads, a different oil sending unit boss, and bosses for the oil cooler.

Hummer H3 Alpha 5.3

The H3 oil pan (PN 12614821) is commonly referred to as the LH8. Originally designed for the Hummer H3 with the LS 5.3 engine, it has become a very popular stock oil pan for A-Body swaps. First available in late 2007, its measurements caused quite a stir in the LS-swap community because the long 13-inch shallow front section allows this pan to clear most stock GM crossmembers without modification. Again, though, this pan has a 7½-inch-deep rear sump, making it hang about 1½ to 2 inches below the crossmember. A stock suspension on a car would be able to clear the road, but any lowering and this pan could be an issue. Chevrolet Performance based its muscle car LS swap pan on the LH8 design and its application to A-Bodies.

Corvette LS2

The LS2 Corvette oil pan (PN 12581810), not to be confused with the LS7 pan, possibly fits some A-Body models. The 5-inch-deep rear sump certainly clears the road, but the 13½-inch length of the sump prevents this pan from being used in most A-Body chassis. It can be modified for a particular vehicle and could save some cash. The relatively flat and square rear sump area makes the pan easy to modify, but it still might not be worth it to buy this pan.

Corvette LS7 Dry-Sump

The LS7 is a specialized pan that fits only the LS7; it's a dry-sump oiling system and requires a lot of special consideration. If you are swapping an LS7 into a GM A-Body, an aftermarket oil pan is required. Modifying the stock pan is not a simple task because of the internal oil routing design. ATS offers a sheet-metal oil pan for

Inside the 2010–up Camaro is this oil pan, used under LS3 and LSA engines. It has provisions for mounting an oil cooler. Its odd shape makes it a tricky pan for swappers. Improved Racing makes this pan with internal baffling. (Photo Courtesy Improved Racing)

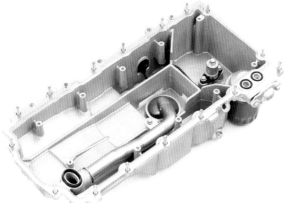

The wet-sump LT1 pan features a large sump that simply does not fit the A-Body chassis. To use the stock pan, the crossmember has to be modified. The issue is the integral pick-up that is cast into the pan and the oval-shaped pick-up seal. (Photo Courtesy General Motors)

the LS7 that fits the first-generation F-Body (1967–1969 Chevy Camaro/Pontiac Firebird). Although this pan was designed for the F-Body, it also fits 1964–1972 A-Bodies.

GTO LS3

The GTO oil pan is a front-sump design and, therefore, not compatible with the A-Body.

2010-up LS3/LSA Camaro

The fifth-generation Camaro uses a different oil pan than the fourth-generation F-Body. The newest Camaro pan has a long rear sump that doesn't clear the front crossmember on the A-Body, leaving it out as a versatile pan for swappers.

LS9 Corvette ZR1

Like the LS7, the LS9 in the ZR1 Corvette is a dry-sump design, yet it can be retrofitted to other blocks.

However, after the time and money spent adapting this factory pan, you could have bought an aftermarket dry-sump pan that likely better fits the application at a lower cost.

Gen V Oil Pans

Unlike previous engine designs, the Gen V pan uses an integrated pick-up tube. The pan does not have a gasket, and the pick-up port is oval, not round. This makes both aftermarket reproduction and modification quite difficult. Aftermarket pans are being developed but are not currently available. Three versions (LT1, LT4, and L86 truck) of oil pans for the LT-series engines are currently offered.

LT1

The 2014 LT1 oil pan resembles the fourth-generation F-Body pans, so it does not readily fit the 1964–1972 A-Body. Adapting it to this platform is challenging because of the engine setback. To clear the crossmember, the LT1 needs to sit about 1 inch back, near the stock location of the engine-to-transmission mating surface. With a late-model transmission (4LXX or later), the transmission hits the tunnel, requiring serious modification. Moving the engine forward requires modification of the crossmember.

The LT1 crate engines come with a liquid-to-liquid oil cooler that bolts to the side of the pan/block and uses engine coolant to control the oil temperature. The crate does not come with required fittings to make this functional. You need a special coolant line for the block to the cooler and a line for the cooler to the radiator.

Although not inexpensive, they are compatible with a GM A-Body, but you need an available port on the radiator. The components cost about $200 through online GM parts vendors (dealer-only items). For about $25, you can remove the cooler and install the block-off plate and engine block plug, which are also dealer items.

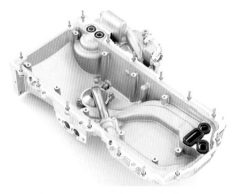

The dry-sump pan has a shallower sump that sets back farther, but the oil cooler is bolted to the side of the pan, which doesn't clear the frame on the side. The cooler can be removed. (Photo Courtesy General Motors)

Oil Pan Considerations

One more note on factory oil pans: You can swap pans from engine to engine, but you need to pay attention to a few items. The pick-up tube and windage tray go with the oil pan, not the engine. These items are a matched set, so any time you swap the oil pan, you need to swap the correct tube and windage tray as well. In addition, DOD engines have an oil-pressure bypass valve built into the oil pan. If you are not using the DOD system, it doesn't matter. But if you have a DOD engine and plan to use the DOD system, you need an oil pan that has the bypass valve.

One of the benefits of an aftermarket pan is that many of them have internal baffles designed to keep the pick-up tube surrounded by oil all the time, even under severe G-forces. The baffles trap the oil so it doesn't slosh to one side of the pan, potentially uncovering the pick-up tube. You can install an improved racing baffle on a modified factory pan that has an internal baffle.

The F-Body oil pan is one of the biggest culprits for high-G oil starvation. Improved Racing designed a bolt-in baffle for the F-Body pan (it also offers these for the Gen V Camaro and GTO pans) that is a direct bolt-in; no welding required. By reducing the sloshing and aeration of the oil, the engine can maintain oil pressure without oil starvation.

You can install a bypass adapter. This boss can also be swapped out for an oil-cooler bypass regulator.

LT4 Dry-Sump

The supercharged 6.2-liter LT-series engine is also a dry-sump design. The shallow front section of the dry-sump pan should clear the 1964–1972 A-Body chassis. The biggest problem with this pan is all the lines that have to be run. It is certainly feasible, however.

L86 5.3 and 6.2 Truck

This oil pan has a large rear sump and a very deep front section. This is not a good swap pan.

Aftermarket Gen III/IV Oil Pans

With so many options and potential pitfalls, many builders choose an aftermarket oil pan that

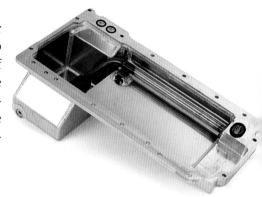

The first LT1 swap pan was recently released. This fabricated aluminum pan from BRP Hot Rods designed specifically for Tri-Five Chevys and 1964–1972 GM trucks should fit the A-Body chassis. Actual fitment depends on your engine package and motor mount adapters. (Photo Courtesy BRP Hot Rods)

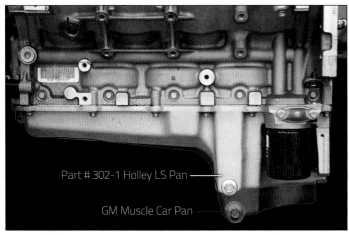

Holley came to the oil pan market with the LSX retrofit pan. This aluminum oil pan features a stock-style oil filter mount and has adequate clearance for most popular swaps. It is also a beefy design, with thick casting ridges for strength. Here you see a comparison between the Holley pan and the Chevy Performance muscle car pan. The biggest concern is that the Chevy Performance pan hangs too low to be safe on most cars. The Holley pan fixed that. (Photo Courtesy Holley Performance Products)

Mast Motorsports offers a cast LS swap pan (left). The front sump section is slightly lower, allowing a little more clearance for the tie-rods on A-Body frames. The Holley pan (PN 301-1, right) is the early version; a newer version has more clearance on the front sump. The front profile is the key; note that the Holley pan is slightly taller in the front. Whether this is an issue depends on the motor mounts and adapters.

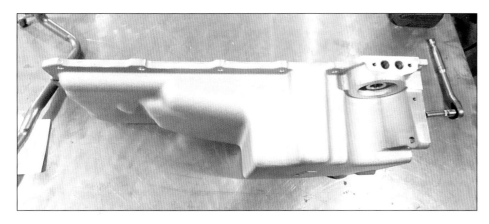

The newest version of the Holley pan (PN 301-2) has the shorter front sump section. It was designed specifically for LS swaps into GM A- and F-Body cars using Hooker adapters.

Installing a new pan is not as simple as just bolting it on. All LS pans have specific pick-up tubes and windage trays, each matching the pan, so make sure you have the matching tray and tube. This Holley pan may require a small notch on the windage tray to fit some engines.

Inside the Holley pan, install a sump cover. Make sure you use medium threadlocker on the bolts to keep them from coming loose.

This sump cover helps keep the oil from sloshing around, keeping the pick-up covered in oil at all times.

The final step is to install the pan on the block with a new gasket. LS oil pan gaskets are reusable if they are not bent.

The inner tie-rods present a clearance issue with many swap projects. The grease fitting tends to hit the pan. The severity of the interference depends on the tie-rod and the height of the engine. This is a common problem on all A-Body vehicles.

The Canton aluminum drag race oil pan for LS engine swaps fits GM A-, F-, and Y-Body cars as well as 1970s Nova X-Body cars. It is an aluminum sheet-metal pan with trap door baffles for oil control. The required remote filter adapter is included. (Photo Courtesy Canton Racing Products)

This Moroso pan is similar to the shallow Moroso pan and fits GM A-Body cars. It features a deep-angled front sump section and expedites the oil's return to the sump. (Photo Courtesy Moroso)

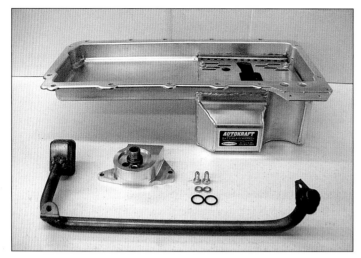

AutoKraft uses stamped steel and sheet-metal fabrication on its LS swap oil pan. Designed for road race applications, it uses a four-corner baffling design to maintain proper oil levels. It also can be installed with the oil filter adapter, allowing the filter to remain in the stock location. (Photo Courtesy AutoKraft)

For the LS7, ATS offers this pan for the 1967–1969 F-Body cars with the ATS engine mounts. If you flip the ATS engine mounts upside-down, this pan can be used in 1964–1967 GM A-Body cars as well. (Photo Courtesy American Touring Specialties)

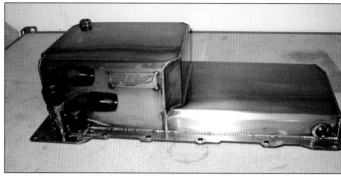

The ATS sheet-metal road race pan works well with the GM A-Body cars when used with ATS engine mounts. The internal baffling controls oil slosh in hard cornering. (Photo Courtesy American Touring Specialties)

The ATS baffling design keeps the oil directly around the oil pickup, ensuring that there is no loss of oil pressure. (Photo Courtesy American Touring Specialties)

Improved Racing's bolt-in baffles can be purchased for the stock 2010 Camaro pan, GTO, and F-Body pans to add oil control when using a stock pan. (Photo Courtesy Improved Racing)

fits specific vehicles. Many versions are available, but most are based on two platforms: the first-generation F-Body 1967–1969 Chevy Camaro and Pontiac Firebird version and the 1965–1972 GM A-Body version for cars such as the Chevy Chevelle, Pontiac GTO, Buick GS/Skylark, and Oldsmobile Cutlass/442.

Most fabricated (meaning welded steel or aluminum, not cast) aftermarket oil pans require the use of a remote oil filter. This is sometimes seen as a major drawback for some builders because it means finding a place to locate the filter and run the lines. This is not always the case, however, as several aftermarket pans such as the Holley LSX-swap cast-aluminum pan maintain the pan-mounted filter. If an oil pan fits the first-gen F-Body, in most cases it clears the A-Body chassis as well.

Oil Coolers

Oil temperatures are important, especially if you are road racing or run a supercharger/turbo on your LS. Maintaining proper engine oil temperature is critical to both the life of the engine and the usable life of the oil. Chevrolet suggests running your engine oil between 220 and 240 degrees at full warm-up. This is higher than the previously acceptable range of 190 to 220, and is a point of contention among experts.

That doesn't change the fact that temperatures over 250 degrees begin to break down the oil, dramatically reducing its usable life. Colder oil temps are also an issue and rob your engine of power. LS engines run tighter tolerances than the old small-block Chevy; the cooler the oil, the thicker it is. That means there is less oil inside the bearings, increasing friction and costing more power. Heat

the oil up a little more and the oil flows better, reducing the friction and freeing up a little extra power, not to mention adding life to the engine.

Another side-effect of running the engine oil too cool is the lack of sufficient burn-off temperature. Engine oil becomes contaminated with fuel and water through condensation. When the oil reaches 200 degrees, the fuel and water begin to burn off. Although this is necessary for a naturally aspirated engine, it is critical for a turbocharged engine, as the turbos are cooled through the engine oil system. Water and fuel in the oil can waste turbo bearings in a hurry.

Adding an oil cooler to your LS engine during the swap project is an easy way to maintain the correct engine oil temperatures, but simply adding an inline cooler is not the answer. If oil is allowed to flow through the cooler, it takes longer to warm up and runs cooler overall.

The key to a proper oil cooling system is thermostatic bypass. All factory LS engine oil pans have an oil bypass port built right into the side of the pan above the oil filter. These ports can be used for the oil cooler lines (as well as the oil pressure sending unit), or you can use an oil filter sandwich-type adapter. Several companies make oil cooler adapters for these factory ports.

A thermostatic bypass port allows engine oil to circulate through the cooler only after it reaches a certain temperature. It allows oil to warm up faster, and if it cools too quickly in the cooler, the bypass closes, maintaining a consistent minimum temperature. These types of valves can be found in adjustable versions; they are usually sold in static ranges, typically opening at 180 degrees and becoming fully open at 200 degrees.

Several newer Gen III/IV LS engines have oil coolers built into them, namely the high-performance and some Vortec heavy-duty applications. If you choose to run an aftermarket oil pan with a remote oil filter, the plumbing allows you to add an inline cooler. Thermostatic bypasses are available for this design as well.

It is usually easy to locate the cooler because it's often mounted in front of the radiator or A/C condenser. But they don't have to go there; you can mount the cooler just about anywhere it can receive the airflow. "Hot rod"-style coolers mount on the frame, for example; some even have 12-volt fans for forced-air cooling. There are a lot of options, but the simplest solution is a radiator front mount.

As previously mentioned, many aftermarket oil pans do not have factory-style oil filter mounts, only ports for the oil feed and return lines. This means you must run a remote oil filter. Locating the oil filter can be a challenge in many applications, but it is a necessary component. If you use an oil cooler, the filter can be in the same location. The key here is that you want easy access to the filter and protection from road debris. If the filter is hanging too low, it could become damaged, leaving you with a shattered engine. The lines for the oil filter do not have to be high-pressure, but braided lines certainly look cool and reduce the risk of leaks or blowouts from cut or damaged lines.

An important note for the installation of a remote filter on LS engines: The ports are not labeled and some oil pans do not include instructions indicating which port is the pressure and which is the return. The pressure port is the front (toward the belts) port, with the return being the rearmost port.

Performance Project: Modifying a Crossmember for Oil Pan Clearance

When fitting an LS engine in a stock chassis, a stock oil pan and stock crossmember can be modified to the chassis in most cases. The front engine crossmember is large enough to support significant modification, provided the removed section is boxed in to eliminate flex points. To reinforce and strengthen the engine crossmember, cut a small notch on the back side of the crossmember and fill it with 10-gauge (1/8-inch) steel while allowing the engine to sit in place. The front brake crossover line also requires relocation, so you need to simply reroute the brake line using a brake line bending kit.

Until the aftermarket releases a suitable replacement oil pan for the LT-series engines, installing one into a GM A-Body chassis requires modifying the front crossmember. This pro-cess is also useful for LS swaps using certain stock oil pans. Each install requires different dimensional cuts. When you make this modification, you cut the crossmember to match your particular installation parameters, including the height and lateral location of the engine itself.

To begin, the engine must be placed in the vehicle where you want it. The best method is to use an engine hoist with an adjustable-angle attachment mounted to the engine. Lower the engine as far as you can until it hits. In the case of the 1971 Buick GS shown here, I installed a set of Dirty Dingo sliding motor mounts, and set the engine on the mounts in the rearmost posi-tion. Having the engine in the car allows you to mark the cross-member for the oil pan location, removing much of the guesswork.

1 *With the engine in position, you can see where the pan hits the chassis. I used a gold sharpie to outline the pan on the crossmember and then removed the engine.*

2 *The sharpie marks the outline of the pan. You don't want to cut right on the lines, you need to add at least 1/4 inch for suitable clearance. I added 1/2-inch clearance to have plenty of adjustment.*

3 *You can use whatever method you want to cut the metal; I used a plasma torch to make quick work of it. You can also use a pnuematic rotary cutting tool.*

4 *Inside the crossmember I found some scale and rust. It didn't degrade the integrity of the frame, but I took the opportunity to remove it. I killed the rust and painted it to protect it from future rusting.*

5 *Grinding is messy business. I have found that the flap-wheel-style grinding discs are much better for this type of work. They leave a better finish and don't scar the surrounding metal. They are also available in smaller diameters to better access tight spots. After I cleaned up the jagged edges from the plasma cuts, I moved on to the process of making the boxing plates.*

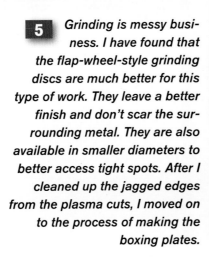

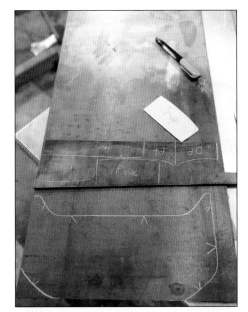

6 I used cardboard to trace the shapes of each section for the boxing plates. I set the depth to the lowest section of the crossmember, specifically the rearmost edge. I then transferred each pattern to 1/8-inch steel plate.

7 I used a bandsaw to cut out the plates, but you can use a rotary tool, plasma torch, or any other suitable tool that provides clean cuts. Don't forget to mark each piece because they are side-specific.

8 Often a little trimming and adjusting is required for each piece to fit perfectly. Once set, I tacked each piece into place.

9 *The side plates are trickiest, as there are several angles to match up. Just a light tack weld is best because you may need to tweak the fitment.*

10 *I used a welder's magnet to hold the bottom of the boxed section in place and tacked it in as well.*

11 *After a few stitch welds to hold the pieces together, I used a hammer to convince each side piece to conform to the natural shape of the crossmember.*

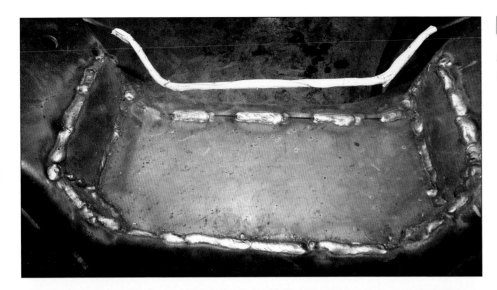

12 I finish-welded the entire box with 1-inch-long stitch welds to reduce warping. Continue the welds until all seams are fully welded.

13 I dressed the welds with the flap disc (80-grit). These discs work well because they don't grind grooves into the metal. Instead they leave a smooth surface, which means less finish work. My frame-boxing project is finished. Because this is a frame-off build, once all the mock-up is done, it all comes apart for the final finish work and paint.

14 I sprayed the metal with etching primer to keep it from rusting. This is an important step because fresh welds flash rust almost instantly. The primer keeps the rust at bay and you can even do body work over it without any issues.

15 *I finished off the notch with some semi-gloss black paint. Once painted, the notch looks pretty good.*

Using a sharpie, I marked the crossmember around the oil pan, noting its placement and a few measurements made to add the 1/2-inch desired clearance. The sliding mounts adjust 2 inches, so the front of the pan could move as much as 2 inches from its standard location. To accommodate for engine twist and movement, I added a minimum of 1/2-inch clearance on all sides of the pan, so I had ample room for adjustment when installing the engine.

There are several ways to cut out the steel. I chose to use a plasma torch because it's quick, easy, and produces clean cuts. Another option is to use an angle grinder with a cut-off wheel. Once I removed the offending steel, I reinstalled the engine to check the fit. This time, the engine set in place with the mounts slid fully forward, and the oil pan had plenty of clearance.

With a large section removed, the crossmember has now lost a good deal of structural integrity. If this were left as is, the crossmember could flex or even collapse. To build strength back into the crossmember, I welded a 1/8-inch steel plate onto the crossmember and boxed-in the notched section; this effectively eliminated the potential flex points.

To correctly complete this procedure, the best method is to use poster board to create patterns for each steel plate piece. You must decide whether to place each piece on the inside or outside of the cut. Adding the piece to the outside reduces clearance and requires a better initial cut of the crossmember. Attaching it on the inside yields a better fit and finish, but also requires a more precise cut on the new pieces. I chose the inside for a better finish.

Another option is to leave the floor of the crossmember open. I did not go this route, preferring the fully-boxed application, and made a new flat floor to complete the box work on the notch, which more closely resembles the factory look and design.

Once the templates were made, I traced them onto the steel (1/8-inch) and used a bandsaw to cut out the steel patch plates, but you can also use a plasma torch or cut-off wheel to complete the procedure. The bandsaw allows for a more accurate cut. Be sure to label each piece for placement as it is cut so that it does not become mixed up with other pieces.

I used a grinder to clean up the edges of the crossmember before the final fitment of the boxing. Plasma cutting leaves slag on the edges and is not always perfectly flat. Clearing off any jagged edges makes for a better fit and less clean up after welding.

The welding step takes a bit of patience because the pieces may not fit together perfectly at first. You may have to do some trimming or adjust the placement slightly as you go. I recommend using small welding magnets to hold each piece in place and help you put all the pieces in at once to check the overall fit. Once you are satisfied with the fit of the panels it is time to weld them into place.

I put each piece in place with one or two tack welds. Small gaps of less than 1/8 inch are acceptable here and there, but you need to avoid big gaps or separation between the pieces of the crossmember itself because this compromises strength. I laid the floor of the box into the opening before the side pieces. After each piece was tacked in place, I lifted the floor section into position with a magnet and tacked it as well. With all the tack work done, I fully welded the boxing with a MIG welder.

The steel is thick enough to run longer beads; I welded each section in 1- to 2-inch beads. In a couple of problem areas the flat plate didn't match the contour of the original crossmember. I remedied this with a few hits from a ball-peen hammer. This is necessary on most fabrication jobs. To reduce warping, I moved the welding to opposite sections for every couple of inches of weld.

After the welds had cooled, I used a flap-style grinding pad to dress the welds. Be careful to not dig into the metal or grind too far into the weld, weakening the seam. Dressing the welds makes the modification look better and helps you find any pinholes or sections you missed while welding. To fix these issues, just hit it with the welder and dress it down.

Once you are satisfied with the way the welds look, you can move on to installing the engine. On the Buick shown here, I dressed the welds flush and smooth, but a few spots still need attention.

ACCESSORY DRIVES AND COOLING SYSTEMS

GM's stock accessory drives for the LS engine were designed to fit in late-model vehicles with modern frames and spacing. Depending on which accessory drive you have, clearance may or may not be an issue. However, the A/C compressor constantly presents a clearance problem and typically needs to be mounted low on the passenger's side of the engine. It tends to hit the frame rail or the upper A-arm on the suspension at this location. Again, it all depends on the chassis and drive system you are using.

General Motors took a completely different approach to accessory location and fit with the LT1 than with the LS-series engines. The water pump is offset to the passenger's side with a high-mount alternator and a low-mount A/C compressor. The power steering and A/C compressor do not interfere with the frame, but the stock drive does not work for A-Body vehicles.

On the other side of the engine, the power steering and alternator placement must be checked because often there are clearance problems. The stock recirculating ball steering gear box can get in the way of the alternator and power steering placement. Each chassis is different and each accessory drive is different. However, there are simple solutions for awkward accessory drive placement.

Specific stock accessory drives work on specific chassis. If you purchased a used engine, you need compatible drive parts. Several options are available if the drive system doesn't fit your car. One is a stock drive that fits your chassis, but these can be difficult to find, especially the older 1998–2002 F-Body drives. Aftermarket drive kits are available that relocate the offending components and add some flash to your install. The final solution, relocating the problem component with a home-fabricated bracket, requires a little more ingenuity and fabrication.

Swapping an LS into an A-Body imposes a few limitations in the

The F-body water pump features a pulley bell that is rounded on the front with a short snout at the tip. Corvettes and some others use the short pump style, which features a flat-faced pulley.

The crankshaft pulleys must match the water pump and accessories. These pulleys are for the LT-series engines, but the features are similar. The pulley on the left is for trucks, and the one on the right is for Corvettes.

accessory drive, mostly for the A/C compressor. Vehicles that do not run A/C and/or power steering are certainly easier to fit and modify than ones requiring all the accessories. Keep that in mind when choosing your accessory drive. An alternator alone is much easier to relocate than three components.

The accessory drives on Gen III/IV engines are interchangeable throughout the product line. However, each accessory drive is based on two components: the water pump and the harmonic dampener or harmonic balancer. LS engines are internally balanced, so it is technically a harmonic dampener, but it's commonly referred to as a balancer. The crank pulley is part of the dampener, but they are one piece, in contrast to a separate pulley that bolts to the balancer.

Three balancer designs are available for LS engines: Corvette, F-Body, and C/K truck styles. The Corvette (Y-Body and CTS-V) dampener is the shortest of the three, placing the drive belt close to the engine. The F-Body (also GTO) dampener is

3/4 inch longer than the Corvette engine's. The C/K (GM truck engines 4.8-, 5.3-, and 6.0-liter) unit is 1-1/2 inches longer than the Corvette unit. This correlates to the water pump as well. Each intended drive system uses a specific water pump, and they vary among the years.

The three water pump offset options are the 1998–2002 F-Body, Corvette, and C/K trucks. Within these groups are subgroups. The F-Body water pump remained the same throughout its production run from 1998 to 2002.

The Corvette (also GTO and CTS-V) in 2004 used one water pump design with some internal differences. The 2005-up Corvette/GTO water pump for the LS2, LS7, and LS3 used the same offset but contained a different internal design. The LS1/LS3 pumps are interchangeable; the LS3 pump uses a lighter pulley, with about 4 pounds of weight savings.

The same story goes for the C/K truck pumps. The 1999–2005 trucks use a specific water pump, but in 2007 the design changed to DOD. Not all 2007 C/K engines use this pump. The offset remains the same as on the early pumps, but you would not want to swap a DOD pump onto a non-DOD engine.

LT Engine Series

The 2014–up LT-series engines are different from the LS-series. Currently there are two distinct setups: car and truck. Like the LS-series, there is a car water pump and crank pulley, and a separate design for the trucks. None of the LT-series engines use a power steering pump, so the factory accessory drive is only good for non–power steering vehicles. You can fabricate a power steering pump bracket, or you can purchase a new accessory drive.

Vehicle Fitment with Stock Accessory Drives

Factory accessory drives are a good budget option for LS swaps in A-Body cars; the trick is finding one that fits your application and configuration. Most stock drives work in A-Body cars without A/C; the compressor tends to get in the way.

C5 Corvette

The C5 Corvette (Y-Body) accessory drive fits and clears the stock chassis and stock chassis components with most motor mount adapters. The C5 uses a variable clutch speed compressor that rides low on the smaller secondary four-rib belt. Depending on the motor mounts, you may have clearance issues. A Sanden 508 A/C compressor on an S&P bracket positions the compressor forward to clear the chassis and puts the A/C compressor on the larger six-rib belt. This drive places the A/C compressor low and pushed back on the passenger's side, the power steering pump mounts in front of the driver-side cylinder head, and the alternator rides up and over the power steering pump.

You can run other accessory drives in these cars, but the engine crossmember must be notched to clear the A/C compressor, and the alternator hits the frame and steering gear box in most cases. A rack-and-pinion conversion simplifies the installation.

F-Body

This drive system places the A/C compressor very low and tight to the block, with the A/C centerline just below the center of the crank. The alternator is tucked-up to the left of the crank pulley and the power steering pump is mounted directly above the alternator. The A/C compressor location hits the passenger-side crossmember.

With this 1998–2002 LS1 F-Body drive system, the accessories have a somewhat tight fit to the engine. The A/C compressor and alternator can be difficult to fit to the chassis.

Here is a 2005–2006 GTO accessory drive. The A/C compressor hangs fairly wide, so it is somewhat difficult to fit between the frame rails. (Photo Courtesy Blane Burnett)

The CTS-V drive system pulls the A/C compressor in tighter to the block than on the GTO and uses the shortest crank pulley design for the most room. (Photo Courtesy Blane Burnett)

Vortec Truck

The Vortec truck accessory drive positions the A/C compressor just below the crank centerline, tucked-in really tight to the passenger's side of the block, making it difficult to use on a GM A-Body without modifying the crossmember. The power steering pump mounts tight to the block, midway between the crank and water pump. The alternator is out of the way at the top of the engine, above the power steering pump, next to the throttle body. The alternator could prove to be problematic for hood clearance if your engine is raised for oil pan–to-steering clearance.

CTS-V

The CTS-V drive also positions the A/C pump tight to the block (lower passenger's side) and uses the short pump design, maximizing the radiator-to-engine clearance. The power steering pump positions midway between the water pump pulley and the throttle-body on the driver's side and allows plenty of hood clearance. The tight and low alternator works well for the A-Body chassis. The CTS-V accessory drive has been used as the starting point for some of the most popular aftermarket systems with the key exception being the A/C placement, which hits the frame on A-Body cars.

Gen V LT

The drive design for the Gen V car works great, until you want A/C. Like most stock drives, the low-mount

A/C is a real problem for the A-Body chassis. Without A/C it fits well. Also, the factory offers no power steering pump option.

Aftermarket Drives

When you factor in all the costs, using the stock accessory drive on your LS is not the most inexpensive solution, but let me be clear, it may be the best solution. The first order of business is to figure out if the stock drive is compatible with an A-Body swap project. The stock drives are as eye pleasing as the aftermarket pieces. Sure, the stock brackets are aluminum and can be polished, which would look nice, but that requires a tremendous amount of work and upkeep. Polished aluminum fades and oxidizes quickly, and requires constant attention to retain a mirror finish unless it is anodized.

Of course, there is no guarantee that the stock drive will fit. Your install depends on the motor mounts you choose and how you set up your engine; there are always tolerances that may not work in some circumstances. For example, stock bellhousing placement can cause crossmember clearance issues. A/C and power steering pump placement can too. An aftermarket accessory drive simplifies the install, removing the guesswork and ensuring that everything clears, provided it is specified for use in A-Body platforms. The Holley Performance and Dirty Dingo drives are very popular because they fit well and look good.

The Holley LSX accessory drive system comes in all three pulley lengths and has several options for positioning the accessories for maximum clearance. It is also available for both the factory R4 A/C compressor and Sanden-style units.

Using the truck balancer, I installed the Holley truck spacer kit for the 5.3-liter in the 1969 Chevelle. The spacers simply mount between the accessory brackets and the engine, placing them at the perfect location.

Installing the brackets is as simple as using the supplied bolts and driving them into the heads. Don't over-torque them, as the threads can strip easily on the aluminum heads. M8 bolts need 18 ft-lbs of torque; M10 bolts need 36 ft-lbs.

This bracket holds the alternator, power steering pump, and one of the idler pulleys. These are available in polished or as-cast finish (shown).

The Holley system uses a GM type-II power steering pump. The supplied bracket secures the pump to the bracket.

When mounting the power steering pump, the single biggest issue is often the fitting for the reservoir feed. Multiple port types include straight and angled tubes and threaded ports. If you have the wrong pump, you can always change the fitting and use press-fit sealant to secure it.

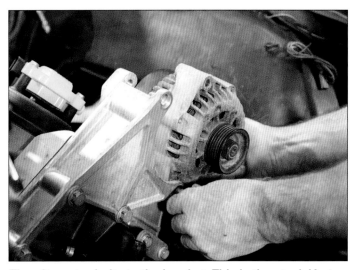

The alternator bolts to the bracket. This is the stock Vortec alternator; it is a direct fit.

I reused the idler from the original Vortec accessory drive. You can also purchase the brackets in a complete kit with the accessories, which is a great way to make sure all the right parts are used.

This system uses the Holley power steering pump pulley to get the correct installation depth. It is a press-fit, so you need the installation tool as well.

The stock idler installs on the upper passenger's side of the water pump. A new belt on the pulleys, and the system is ready to run.

With everything put together, the Holley system fits nicely with no interference issues.

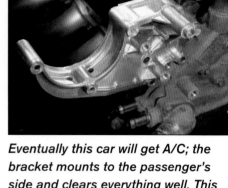

Eventually this car will get A/C; the bracket mounts to the passenger's side and clears everything well. This is for the stock-type compressor. The kit is also available for a Sanden compressor, which is most commonly used for aftermarket A/C systems.

Currently, the only aftermarket drive (Dirty Dingo) for LT-series engines is based on the truck crank pulley, so it must be purchased for Chevrolet Performance crate engines. In addition, the water pump must be swapped out for the C6 Corvette unit, which has a center-mounted pulley. The stock LT pulley is offset.

Cooling Systems

Swapping LS engines into non–V-8 vehicles can raise challenges for the cooling system. The stock copper/brass radiator for a V-8 should be able to cool an LS, but you need to deal with the steam lines. An aftermarket aluminum radiator is an easy solution that handles the load and provides the input for the steam line. These are readily available for all 1964–1972 A-Body platforms. In addition to the radiators, the car Gen III/IV engines were designed for electric cooling fans; only the Vortec engines have mechanical fans.

Radiator

The Gen III/IV engines use a conventional cooling system, so they do not require huge radiators or special metals. What they do require is a radiator that is rated for the job. With the smallest LS engines easily making 300 hp, you don't want to use a stock 4-cylinder or V-6 radiator. Making horsepower means producing

heat as a byproduct, but LS engines are pretty efficient when it comes to managing heat. Considering that most GM A-Body platforms used V-8 engines as the base engine from the factory, and the massive aftermarket that caters to these vehicles, V-8 radiators are easy to find. V-6 A-Bodies need a radiator upgrade. You have some choices though.

The factory copper and brass radiator have a channel like the one on the core (center) top and bottom, and it fits precisely into the radiator mounts on the car. A stock V-8 A-Body radiator can handle the cooling needs of an LS in most instances. The driver-side tank is a little smaller on this 1971 Buick GS radiator. A-Body radiators vary by make and model, but the overall dimensions are very similar.

Aluminum versus Copper: In most vehicles built through the 1970s, OEM radiators are constructed of brass. They are expensive and not the most effective for cooling an engine. Copper quickly absorbs and dissipates heat at a faster rate than aluminum.

Aluminum radiators absorb and dissipate heat quickly, too, but at a slower rate than copper. Aluminum radiators are stronger, so the cooling tubes are made with thinner walls. The radiator can be fitted with more cores and rows than a traditional copper radiator for increased cooling surface area, which in turn increases the cooling capacity. In addition, aluminum is cheaper than brass, which certainly plays a part.

Electrolysis is an important factor to consider when maintaining cooling system health. Any time you have two different metals in a coolant system, there is the potential for electrolysis, which happens when one weaker material is eaten away and deposited on the other. This can be disastrous for an aluminum engine because aluminum is generally the sacrificed material.

When running a copper/brass radiator, these metals have the potential to ruin an aluminum component on the engine.

The simple solution is to install an anode kit in the radiator. Anodes used in machinery and marine applications protect the cooling systems and other components from damage due to electrolysis or coolant additive failure and breakdown. Flex-a-Lite offers a zinc anode kit (PN 32060) for installation as a replacement drain petcock in radiators that are equipped with a 1/4-inch NPT bushing welded into the tank. The anode may also be installed in any 1/4-inch NPT hole that is available in the cooling system. Aluminum parts may disintegrate from electrolysis in the cooling system. The introduction of the zinc anode protects your cooling system from galvanic action because it eats away at the zinc rather than the cooling system.

Coolant: The best coolant for LS engines is a frequent topic of discussion, particularly in engine swaps. GM's DexCool is the factory engine coolant and is recommended by General Motors. That said, those rec-

ommendations are for stock vehicles, using all stock components. The Dex-Cool coolant is specifically designed for aluminum radiators, *not* for copper/brass radiators.

DexCool's harsh and resilient organic acids attach to the solder in copper radiators, rendering them useless. The DexCool coolant also tends to sludge up in the system over time due to contaminants. When swapping an LS engine, most builders suggest flushing the engine with water three or four times until it comes out clear and there are no more hints of orange color.

When the coolant system is clean, add new coolant. Most builders agree that the aftermarket (non–GM brand) orange long-life equivalent works well in systems with copper/brass radiators. The coolant you use must be compatible with both metals. A brand such as Prestone works with both. The typical green antifreeze provides more than adequate performance, as well, so long as you have properly flushed the system.

Inlet/Outlet Positioning: This is a key consideration when buying a radiator. All LS engines have inlet

The biggest issue for aftermarket aluminum radiators is that the core is thicker than the original, so they tend to not fit the stock mounting locations quite as well. You can see that this top cover hits the tank.

The quick solution to this unwanted contact is a piece of hose or foam under the cover to protect the radiator from damage. You can also trim the edges of the cover to lay flat on the radiator. This is a common issue with aftermarket swaps.

Some cars have a wide tray that readily fits a four-core aluminum radiator, while others do not. This 1969 Chevelle does not fit very well, and the lower tray needs to be modified. This varies by make, model, and engine package.

and outlet positions on the driver's side of the engine. In most cases, the easiest solution is to purchase a radiator with passenger-side inlets and outlets. Because there is no mechanical fan in the way, running the upper return hose to the driver's side is simple if your stock radiator has a driver-side upper mount. The lower feed hose is more difficult to cross over to the driver's side, depending on the distance between the engine and radiator. It is possible to move inlets and outlets, but the expense would likely be just as much as purchasing a new radiator.

Aftermarket Offerings: Each of the many aftermarket radiators has its benefits. Quality of the materials and construction are important. Aluminum radiators start at $200 to $250 for an A-Body car, and cost increases from there. A few options are available for ordering a radiator.

The first and simplest is to order an off-the-shelf unit with the inlets and outlets where the manufacturer placed them. New aftermarket radiators that mount in the stock location are available for 1964–1972 A-Body cars.

You can save some cash by purchasing a "custom fit" radiator, typically sold in terms of dimension. For example, a four-core 33-x-18–inch radiator is actually 33 inches wide and 18 inches long. Often these radiators fit in the stock location using the stock or slightly modified mounting hardware and can cost as much as 30 percent less.

Take into consideration that the radiator core support designs vary by brand and year, and Chevelles, Cutlasses, GTOs, and GSs often have different core supports. The 1969-and-older vehicles have side rails on the core support with a shallow lower tray for the radiator supports. This can lead to an aftermarket aluminum radiator sitting higher in the core support than the factory brass/copper radiator. In most cases, even with the "factory fit" type of radiators, the original upper radiator mount (a bolt-on sheet-metal piece) requires modification to fit the taller and thicker aluminum radiators.

The factory V-8 copper/brass radiator measures 18.5 inches tall, 34.5 inches wide, and 3 inches thick. The inlet is on the upper driver's side while the outlet is on the lower passenger's side. Most aluminum stock-fitment replacement radiators for A-Body cars measure 30 to 33.75 inches wide, 18 to 18.75 inches tall, and 2 to 3 inches thick, depending on the number of rows and the tank design.

The fitment issue comes in the design and thickness of the core. The brass/copper core is only 16 inches tall, with a narrow channel measuring 1.25 inches thick added to fit into the mounts. Most aluminum radiators use a full-size 18-inch-plus core, which is also the full thickness of the overall radiator. This means that the

stock rubber isolators do not fit well and the radiator tends to sit higher in the core support, so the upper radiator mount does not fit well.

The options are to cut down the factory isolators or replace them with an analog such as a split rubber hose or bulk rubber pads. The upper radiator cover can be reused as is, modified, or a custom cover made. Most builders simply reuse the stock upper cover with some modification. The upper covers vary by year and original configuration.

Overflow Tank

Depending on the model of car, you may or may not have an overflow tank. Most LS engines function best when the radiator is coupled with a functioning overflow tank that purges excess water to the tank when hot and draws water back into the cooling system when cool. These are readily available in the aftermarket. Some high-end A-Body vehicles, particularly 1971–1972 models, have these tanks from the factory.

Keep in mind that most aftermarket aluminum radiators are about 1.5 inches taller than the factory copper/brass unit. This is universal for direct-fit aluminum A-Body radiators. This places the radiator higher in the core support. Slight modifications to the upper radiator cover may be required.

Water Pump and Neck

The water pump outlet position varies by engine model. The three water pump types are Truck, F-Body, and Corvette. This goes along with the crank pulley depth issue. The truck version is the deepest, followed by the F-Body and then the Corvette (which is the shortest and the pulley is closest to the block). The Corvette and F-Body pumps feature a

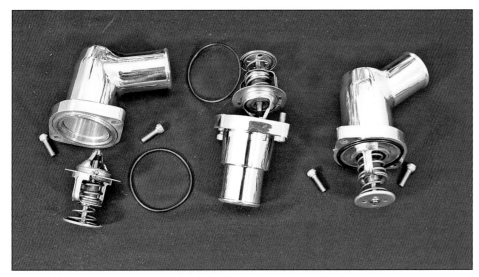

These 45- (right) and 15-degree (left) necks swivel 360 degrees to make swaps a little easier. If the stock neck doesn't properly route the hose to the manifold, you need to look into one of these.

Stock Radiator Hose Fitments

The following are recommendations for stock radiator hose fitments with stock-radiator inlet/outlet locations. These hoses fit 1968–1972 A-Body LS swaps in most configurations.

With Car Pump
Upper: 1998 LS1 Camaro upper hose, no trimming required
Lower: Stock 2000–up truck Vortec (gates 15769077) hose, trimmed to fit

With Truck Pump
Upper: Stock 2000–up truck Vortec, trimmed to fit
Lower: Stock 2000–up truck Vortec (gates 15769077) hose, trimmed to fit

forward-directed output to the upper radiator hose (passenger's side of the engine). Truck pumps direct the output up and out at an angle.

Either pump fits the A-Body chassis; the biggest difference is the crank pulley and the accessory drive being used. Finding the right hoses to fit an LS swap can take time. Keep in mind that your application may vary in respect to engine placement, accessory drive, and radiator. Most parts stores allow hoses to be returned if they are not cut or installed. Don't modify the hose unless you are will-

ing to eat the cost should it not work.

Although a stock black rubber hose may be your choice, flexible aluminum and stainless steel hose kits are available. I used the Summit Racing polished stainless steel kit (PN SUM-390036) on the 1971 Buick GS LT swap featured in this book. It solves the problem of both fitment and accessory clearance and brings a good look to the engine bay. The hoses can be painted, polished, powder coated, or even anodized to match the rest of the underhood trim. The tubing comes in bulk

length; you cut it to fit the application. And because it is bendable, it can be reused if a later change is necessary.

The stock cast-aluminum water neck points at a 90-degree angle to the passenger side, and it fits the A-Body chassis perfectly with the correct hoses. The heater hose fittings point straight toward the passenger-side inner wheel well with plenty of room for the hoses to connect without any modification. Aftermarket straight and 360-degree swivel water necks with either a 15- or 45-degree outlet are alternatives to the stock cast water neck.

The one you choose depends on the radiator outlet position and cooling fan. A mechanical fan with a driver-side radiator outlet requires routing the lower hose under the engine, whereas an electric fan allows the hose to run in front of the engine. Many owners opt for an electric fan because it does not create parasitic drag on the engine. Each water neck must match the water pump design, 1998–2003 and 2004–up. Because there is no mechanical fan to get in the way, you can easily run a lower radiator hose to the driver-side outlet instead of having to buy a new radiator.

Steam Lines

A pair of steam lines that route from the cylinder heads through the throttle body and on to the radiator is a unique feature of LS engines. This line circulates warm coolant through the throttle body to warm the intake charge on cold days and ensures that no air is in the cooling system. It must also be routed to the return tank on the radiator. You have three ways to accomplish this.

The first is to use a traditional

LS engines have steam lines. These lines purge air from the system and feed warm air to the throttle body. These lines must be connected to the radiator. (Photo Courtesy Blane Burnett)

This kit from Summit Racing converts factory steam fittings to AN-style with AN-to-barbed line hoses. (Photo Courtesy Summit Racing)

If your radiator does not have an extra input for the steam lines, adding this line to the water pump is an alternative that also approves the appearance of the engine bay a little. With the pump off the engine, you drill a pilot hole in the flat spot and tap it for a hose fitting.

routing pattern and run a line from the driver-side cylinder head to the return tank on the radiator. The second is to drill and tap the top of the water pump with a 1/4-inch tap, install a 90-degree pipe fitting, and route the steam lines to the top of the water pump. This option certainly results in a cleaner look, but requires more work. As a bonus, if aluminum or stainless steel hard line is used, the lines could be polished, adding some flash to a very utilitarian function. The third solution is to splice a T-fitting into the heater hose, routing the steam line to it instead of the radiator.

Several companies such as Holley Performance and Summit Racing offer steam line kits. These kits include aluminum block mounts and

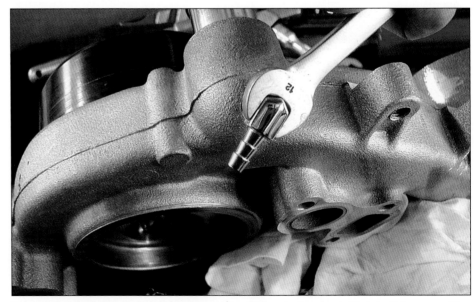

The drilled full-size hole must match the fitting being installed. In this case, it's 3/8 inch.

AN hoses and fittings to eliminate the factory lines. This allows you to customize the routing for your installation.

LT1 Cooling System

The cooling system on Gen V LT1-series engines is somewhat different from those on Gen III/IV engines. First, there are no steam lines on the LT1. Second, the factory temperature gauge mounts in the water pump itself. For A-Body cars, the offset pump accessory drive does not work well. This requires changing to an LS-type water pump using Dirty Dingo conversion mounts. These mounts provide the location for the factory temperature sensor as well as an additional port for a second sensor for aftermarket gauges, fan control, etc.

Electric fans are a must for most LS engines. Saving the original radiator and fan from the donor car is always a viable option. This aftermarket fan from Flex-a-Lite has the necessary shroud built in. (Photo Courtesy Flex-a-Lite)

Electric fans require temperature sensors. This kit simply sits between the tubes and fins. Some electronic control modules (ECMs) have a fan trigger wire that you can use to turn on the fan.

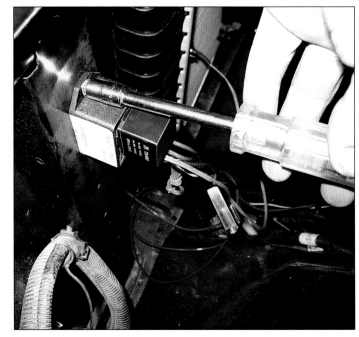

To control the fan, a rheostat control mounts next to the radiator. This box can install anywhere; closest to the radiator is best. Once it is set, you don't need to touch it again.

This thermostat (more accurate than a fin-type) installs directly in place of the petcock.

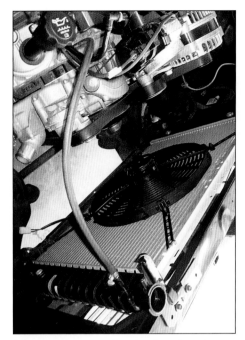

This is an example of a fan that does not use a shroud. Due to its design, air from the fan does not reach much of the radiator. The only time air passes through the radiator is when the car is moving. A shroud ensures more air passes through the radiator when idling, an important feature for city drivers.

Some 1999–2005 Vortec 5300 5.3-liter engines used mechanical fans (shown). However, you can convert them to electric fans. A traditional fan controller such as the Flex-a-Lite or rheostat device must be used to turn on the fan because the ECM doesn't have the wiring or the programming (which could also be added and an aftermarket harness used).

Electric Fan

An electric fan must be used on Gen III/IV (except for 5.3 1999–2005 Vortec) engines because they do not have provisions for a mechanical fan. You have many options for electric fans, both stock and aftermarket, and each fan requires custom fitting to the radiator. For the budget-minded builder, reusing a stock radiator fan is an inexpensive option. Most salvage yards give away stock fans (and maybe the radiator) when you buy a complete engine. Because the Gen III/IV platform is relatively new, there is plenty of life left in the fan motor. Of course, new fans have guarantees and can be configured to your needs.

With an electric fan, correct installation is essential. If the electric fan is not installed correctly (with an electric fan shroud), the fan is not able to draw air through the entire radiator and lose efficiency. The engine reaches operating temperature much faster, maximizing fuel economy because the electric fan is set to run at a determined temperature.

The electric fan may also operate when the engine is off, so the coolant in the radiator cools while the car is sitting. This helps keep the engine in its optimum temperature range when on cruise nights, or for general driving and parking.

When shopping for an electric fan, make sure you purchase one that is designed for high-performance engines and that has a fan shroud, to maximize efficiency. Leading electric fan manufacturers for LS engines include Spal, Maradyne, Flex-a-Lite, Griffin, Auto-Loc Zirgo, and Perma-Cool.

Electric Water Pump

Mechanical water pumps remain the staple for high-performance street cars, and many regard them as strictly drag racing fodder. Meziere Enterprise, for example, offers innovative electric water pumps that deliver superior performance for the street. Meziere pumps are American made and built to the toughest standards in the industry. The company has an excellent reputation due to its two-year, unlimited-mileage guarantee, backed by a money-back full-satisfaction guarantee.

To accurately measure the temperature of the water, you need to install a temperature-sending unit, and the best location is at the back of the passenger-side head. This hole is threaded with a 12-mm plug, so you need an adapter to match the sending unit.

This is a 12-mm sending unit. Most aftermarket gauges use NPT thread, thus the required adapter.

If you don't install the sending unit before you drop in the engine, you might have a problem. The only reason it could be done afterward on this 1969 Camaro is because the A/C box had been shaved. The same issues are present on an A-Body with A/C.

The Meziere pump is available with an idler pulley, so you can retain the serpentine belt system without an idler wheel for race engines. This water pump model fits LS1 through LS8 engines and is suitable for street and drag strip use with its life expectancy of more than 3,000 hours. Each pump is available in show-quality red, black, or blue anodized, polished, or chrome finishes.

Meziere pumps have flow ratings of 42 and 55 gallons per minute; the 42-gpm free-flow rating comes with the heavy-duty engine and the 55-gpm rating comes with the extreme-duty engine. Stainless-steel mounting hardware is included with the lightweight pump. The 1-inch NPT inlet adapters are available (must be purchased separately) for 12AN, 16AN, 20AN, 1¼-inch, 1½-inch, or 1¾-inch slip hose. A 1-inch NPT to 1¼-inch hose outlet adapter is included.

The internal design features a stainless steel large-diameter mainshaft with high-performance ceramic seals. The Meziere pump clears camshaft belt drives, Jesel belt drives, and most blower drives, but spacers are necessary to clear distributor belt drives without the inlet fitting. The fitting must match the size of the lower radiator hose.

Average amperage draw is 6 to 7 amps, and the pump weighs a scant 7 pounds. The standard-duty version is 6.8 inches long from the mounting surface to the tip of the pump, and it weighs only 7.1 pounds. Meziere pumps are also available in 12 or 16 volt. The 42-gpm pump is good up to 650 hp for supercharged, turbocharged, and high-compression applications. High-horsepower applications should use the 55-gpm unit. Heater bypass fittings are included for the 55-gpm water pump, but not on the smaller unit.

If you plan to run aftermarket gauges, you must install an adapter into the block to convert the sending unit to SAE threads. The block has a 12-mm plug on the rear passenger-side head that can be removed to provide the coolant temperature sender location. You drill and tap for pipe thread or fit a simple adapter to the head for converting from 12-mm to 1/8-, 1/4-, 3/8-, or 1/2-inch pipe thread. You need to do this *before* you install the engine in the vehicle; otherwise it is extremely difficult to install the adapter.

Should it be too late to install the adapter, Flex-a-Lite offers an in-line adapter to be placed in the upper radiator hose. The adapter is designed to fit 1½- and 1¾-inch hoses and features two 1/4-inch NPT threaded holes and a brass plug. This makes for a simple way to keep tabs on the coolant temperature.

Autometer offers an LS adapter kit (PN 5284) for use with its gauges. This kit has the correct fittings for the sensors to thread into the LS engine ports as well as a step-down resistor to provide the extra voltage needed to drive an aftermarket tachometer (see Chapter 6 for more information).

Performance Project: Adding Power Steering to a 2014-up LT-Series Engine

The 2014-up LT-series engines are significantly different than the Gen III/IV LS series: The LT series features direct injection; the LS has traditional fuel injection. Another significant change, however, can create more issues for the average swap: The LT does not have conventional hydraulic power steering.

Nearly every new GM car and truck uses electric power assist for steering, and therefore there is simply no need for a power steering pump. The sole exceptions are the 2014-up 2500 and 3500 trucks, which use a Hydroboost for the braking system. Instead of adding a power steering pump on LT engines, General Motors chose to reuse the 6.0 LS-series engine in these larger trucks. Eventually, General Motors may install a factory power steering pump system onto the LT, but until then, any power-steering LT swap project needs an aftermarket solution.

Currently, two distinct accessory setups are offered: car and truck. As with the LS series, the car water pump and crank pulley is a different design than the truck's. This benefits the aftermarket, as it provides some options for adding power steering to the accessory drive. Dirty Dingo was the first company to develop and build a power steering retrofit kit for the aftermarket, and it is rather ingenious.

Instead of trying to work with the offset LT water pump, this system uses the older LS1 Corvette center-driven pump with a pair of billet aluminum spacers to replace the stock LT water pump. The LT and LS share the same bolt and gasket configuration, so it is an easy swap. The spacers also provide a mounting point for a temperature sender because the LT block does not have any alternate cooling ports to tap into.

The center-drive pump allows the use of a typical LS accessory pulley system that mounts on the heads and block. Dirty Dingo uses an aluminum plate and spacer design that fits well and looks good on the LT engine. However, this creates spacing of the water pump that requires the use of the truck crank pulley. If you have a Chevrolet Performance LT crate engine, you need to purchase this pulley separately. The pulley is difficult to remove and install, so make sure you use the correct pulley removal tool.

A couple of wiring harness items must be moved as well. Specifically, the cam VVT solenoid must be re-clocked, and a portion of the steel wiring harness sleeve needs to be removed. The alternator moves to the driver's side of the engine, so you may have to re-route or modify the wiring harness to reach the alternator.

This drive system uses either a fourth-generation Camaro Type-II power steering pump with Dirty Dingo's own pulley or a Type-I Saginaw pump (different brackets). To use a Type-II pump, a press-in or thread-in reservoir feed fitting is required for the pump, which Dirty Dingo sells. The kit is also available with GM R4-type A/C brackets, which give you a lot of options when it comes to adding A/C, or no brackets for the A/C, Sanden 508-type A/C compressor brackets. The factory LT-series accessory brackets with A/C do not clear the frame for most GM muscle cars, making this system even more desirable. Dirty Dingo provides multiple listings for belt lengths depending on the options, including alternator pulley and case size, A/C type, and idler pulley location.

I used the system on a new Chevrolet Performance 6.2 LT crate engine that was being swapped into a 1971 Buick GS convertible. The Dirty Dingo kit works on the smaller 5.3 L83 version as well. Dirty Dingo is working on a version for the LT4 and V-6 LT series. Installation is straightforward; I was able to complete the install in about 2 hours with all the parts on the bench and the engine out of the car. If the engine is in the chassis, it takes longer.

1 *The stock LT-series water pump sits toward the passenger's side. This is not conducive to adding a power steering pump. In addition, the A/C compressor hits the frame in most GM muscle cars.*

3 The Dirty Dingo system uses the truck crank pulley that replaces the factory LT1 Corvette pulley. Use the proper pulley removal tool, so you do not damage the crankshaft snout. These pullers are readily available from any parts store.

2 I removed the factory accessory drive and water pump from the LT-1 and exposed the timing cover and cam VVT solenoid.

4 The truck pulley (left) is deeper than the Corvette pulley (right). Plus it has a couple of extra sets of grooves.

5 The VVT sensor interferes with the Corvette LS1 water pump, so it needs to be repositioned. Three bolts hold the solenoid in place. You need to do this before you install the crank pulley.

6 Cut off the upper loop of the wiring frame just below the mounting point. Remove the wire before cutting the bracket.

7 Rotate the solenoid to face down (shown). The two bolts on the passenger's side and top line up, but the lower driver-side bolt does not. Notch the solenoid plate with an angle grinder, rotary tool, or band saw, so you clearly expose the bolt hole in the block. Make sure you smooth out the notch once it has been made. You can then install the bolt and clamp the solenoid on all sides.

8 Torque down the bolts to secure the solenoid and reattach the wiring harness. I added a wire loop to the lower driver-side bolt to secure the wires.

9 Now the new truck pulley can go onto the crank. I used some red Loctite to add an extra layer of protection for the crank bolt, just as the factory did. This is the original crank pulley bolt.

10 Use an impact gun to drive the pulley into place. You have to lock up the flywheel, so an assistant is helpful here. This process took several tries to get it fully seated and torqued to 240-ft lbs. This is a torque-to-yield bolt, so it is not supposed to be reused. Remove the bolt, then install a new bolt, torque to 110 ft-lbs, loosen 360 degrees, and re-torque the bolt to 59 ft-lbs and then 200 degrees of rotation.

11 *Assemble the spacers for the water pump. I installed the Autometer temperature gauge and used thread sealant. I used the supplied metal gaskets to secure the spacer to the water pump. The bolts capture the reusable gaskets and hold everything in place.*

12 *Mount the pump to the block and torque the mounting bolts to 11 ft-lbs. I also installed the factory LT water temperature sensor into the other spacer.*

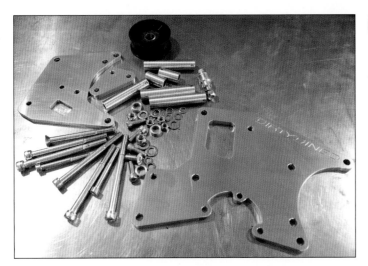

13 *This alternator/power steering bracket kit has several spacers and plates. A couple of spacers are very close in size, but not quite. Each is marked with a letter corresponding to their placement.*

14 *Mount the rear plate to the driver-side cylinder head and torque the bolts to 15 ft-lbs.*

15 Install the lower plate that provides a brace for another bolt and spacer.

16 Install the front plate with the spacers in the correct positions and torque the bolts to 15 ft-lbs.

17 Bolt the original alternator and new Type-II pump into place with the supplied bolts.

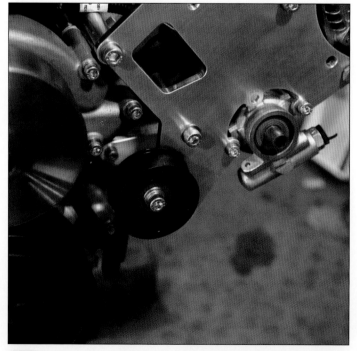

18 Install the lower idler pulley on the bracket as well.

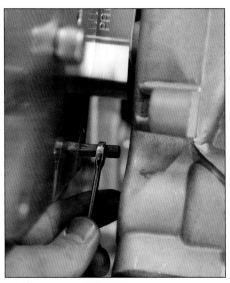

20 *This bolt behind the water pump is difficult to torque down. I used a #3 Phillips bit with a wrench to tighten this one, but you could just mount it before you install the water pump. Dirty Dingo provides instructions for each kit, so it pays to read them ahead of time.*

19 *If you use the A/C bracket, mount it on the passenger-side head. Use several recessed bolts to secure it.*

21 *I installed the front plate and used the supplied spacers along with the tensioner pulley.*

22 *The LT1 Accessory drive kit with power steering has been completely installed. I still need to install the A/C compressor. The LT1 now clears the GM A-body chassis without any issues.*

TRANSMISSIONS

Countless transmission options are available for Gen III/IV engines. From automatics to sticks, stock to modified to aftermarket, there are literally more transmission options than there are versions of the Gen III/IV engine. The LS-series engines share the same basic bellhousing pattern as the original small-block Chevy, so LS engines can be bolted to anything from a 2-speed Powerglide to a 4L80E.

Automatic Transmissions

Bolting an older transmission to an LS engine requires specialized spacers and flexplates because Gen III/IV engines are shorter. If you simply bolt an old-style converter to an LS engine without a spacer, you will have major problems after only a few miles of driving. The pump seal will be ruined and start to leak, causing the pump to fail: The converter won't center on the back of the crank because it does not fit.

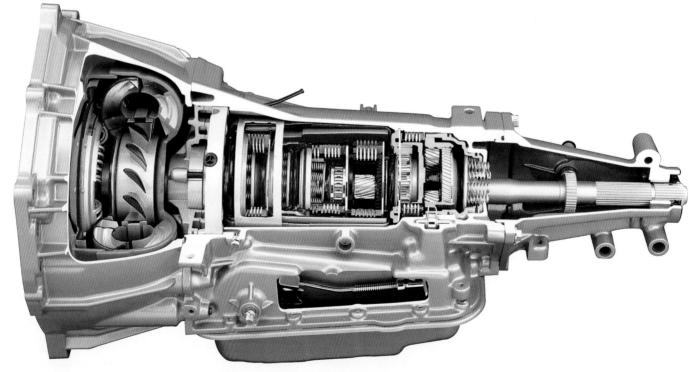

The GM 4L60E is the most popular and most common automatic transmission coupled to Gen III/IV engines because it efficiently transmits power to the driveline, it's strong, and it's reliable. The overdrive is electronically controlled for precise performance. An evolution of the 700R4, the 4L60E is a popular swap transmission. (Photo Courtesy General Motors)

For 1999–2000 Vortec 4.8s 6.0s, GM released this adapter ring. There are two crankshafts for these engines. One is designed for manual transmissions while the other is for automatics. This GM adapter is required to fit the automatic transmission to a manual transmission. The General Motors PN is 12563532.

Flexplates are offered in several versions and one is likely available for your transmission. This stock flexplate fits late-model automatics. Adapting older non-electronic transmissions to an LS requires a spacer ring or adapter flexplate.

To make up for the difference, special conversion flexplates are required. The 6.0-liter Vortec with a 4l80E transmission is the only Gen III/IV engine that accepts an early GM transmission without a flexplate adapter or spacer. These vehicles came with the GM spacer and bolts and the flat factory flexplate.

These are basically the same components needed for an older transmission swap, just performed at the factory.

Several manufacturers offer these components. General Motors sells the spacer plate and longer bolts over the counter. TCI has conversion flexplates for automatic transmissions

and kits that include the spacer and longer bolts. You must use a crankshaft spacer such as the Hughes Performance, TCI, or GM spacer and bolts, or a custom converter must be made with a longer crank hub. Bowtie Overdrives introduced its LS-swap torque converter that eliminates the need to use a spacer; it bolts directly to the stock flexplate.

If installing a used engine, the best solution to the transmission fit

The stock flexplate is curved, not flat like previous GM units, so a special adapter is required when combining the LS with older GM transmissions.

The LT1 bellhousing is similar to the original LS bellhousing. However, you might notice the offset center mounting point because the mechanical fuel pump is mounted in the top of the block.

To mate an LT-series engine with a 4LXX transmission, you need the LT bell-housing. This is a bolt-on piece. Simply unbolt the original bellhousing and bolt on the new one using the same bolts.

On older overdrive transmissions, such as this 200-4R, the TV cable is a crucial component. If it is not set up correctly, the transmission may fail within a few miles. Take time to ensure that it's properly adjusted. TV cable adapter kits for throttle-body or carbed engines each have a specific adjustment process; follow the instructions for your system.

To remove the dangers of the TV cable system, TCI created the Constant Pressure Valve Body. This unit gives the transmission full pressure all of the time, so the shifts are firm and solid, but you can dial it down a bit if needed. The best thing about these valve bodies is that the TV cable is reduced to a shift detent cable, only controlling shift timing. The pressure, which is where the danger is, is out of the equation. Make sure you tighten the bolts to the manufacturer's torque specs. The adapter slips on.

The pan must be removed to replace the valve body, which can easily be done while the transmission is in the car.

The check balls from the old valve body must be retained and reused in the new valve body, but not all of them. Place them in the correct passages according to the instructions and your desired shift characteristics. This part is performed on the bench.

If you must work on the check balls under the car, a little moly grease keeps them in place.

The kit comes with a new backing plate and gaskets. Be sure to save them because the old ones don't work with this valve body. The accumulator spring sits on the plate as shown here.

Carefully align the plate to the transmission and bolt the spring and accumulator back on. This holds up the plate.

Install the valve body and hook up the shifter lever. Bolt the pan on and fill 'er up with your choice of transmission fluid; don't forget the filter. Now the TV cable can be adapted to the throttle body without fear of destroying your transmission.

SWAP LS ENGINES INTO CHEVELLES AND GM A-BODIES: 1964–1972

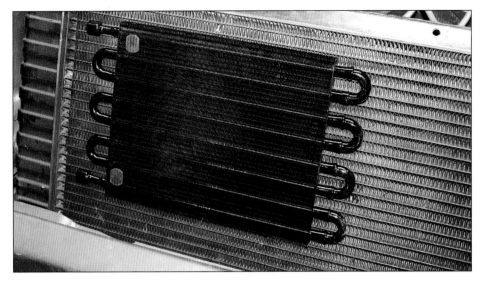

If you do not use a radiator with a built-in transmission cooler, you need one for an automatic. This unit from TCI keeps just about any GM high-performance transmission cool. It sits in front of the radiator.

issue is to use the stock transmission. Then all you must do is fit the transmission to the car.

Adapting the non-electronically controlled 700-R4 and 200-4R requires a little more work. The most important component of these two overdrive transmissions is the throttle-valve cable, or TV cable. This crucial system tells the transmission when to shift and determines the amount of pressure sent to the clutches. If this cable is off even the slightest amount, the clutches do not fully engage, causing the transmission to burn up and eventually fail.

Adapting the TV cable to the throttle body on an LS engine is challenging, and you need to maintain the right geometry. The TV cable system requires a specific percentage of movement at certain points along the travel. The process requires precision because the cable must be at specific positions at specific amounts

If you are using a mechanical speedometer with a newer transmission, adapt the speedometer output to mechanical output. These mechanical speedometer tailshafts are for the 4L60E and 4L65E transmissions.

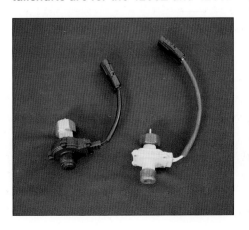

Mechanical/electronic adapters bolt on to the transmission and feed the electronic signal to the computer. A cable then connects to the other side. These are available from Autometer and most gauge suppliers.

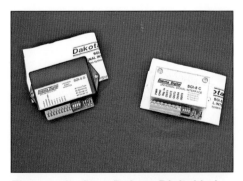

These units from Dakota Digital help convert your transmission's vehicle speed sensor (VSS) signal to non-programmable electronic speedometers if yours is not compatible with the stock VSS signal.

of throttle, and you can't cut a TV cable. If the cable is not the correct length, the transmission will fail. The job demands in-depth knowledge of the TV cable system, and is not suggested for novices. A couple of aftermarket manufacturers, such as Bowtie Overdrives, offer bolt-on solutions for TV cable–to–throttle body conversions.

Another viable alternative to this complicated problem is the TCI Transmission valve body that removes the pressure regulation from the TV system. This valve body keeps the transmission at full-line pressure all the time, ensuring the clutches don't burn up from slipping. The TV cable is then relegated to serve as a speed control for shift points only. A fabricated mount for the TV cable with the precision of the original style is no longer needed, making it much easier to install.

Most Gen III/IV engines in salvage yards, swap meets, and internet sales sites already have a transmission attached. In most cases the transmission is an automatic. The most common GM automatic is the 4L60E (or the 4L65E variant; they are the same dimensionally, but the 1965 version has an extra pinion gear internally), whether the engine came from a car or truck. The larger Vortec engines were typically mated to the 4L80E (and 4L85E variant) automatic transmission. These transmissions require computer controls, which are contained in the factory ECM. They can be purchased separately through the aftermarket for carbureted LS conversions or when an aftermarket electronic fuel injection (EFI) controller is used.

In 2006, General Motors released a couple of 6-speed automatics for its vehicles. The 6L80 and 6L90 transmissions are used in heavy-duty GM

Flywheels are more than just a connector between the transmission and the engine. In fact, they are an integral component to the clutch and can also affect the performance characteristics of the engine. A heavy flywheel holds more inertia for smoother shifts and that's better for street driving. A lighter flywheel allows for quicker revs and shifts, and that's better for road racing. This is a RAM 19.2-pound LS7 flywheel bolted to an LS3. (Photo Courtesy Blane Burnett)

trucks and most of the performance cars. The Sigma platform, which includes the Cadillac CTS line, uses either the 5L40/5L50 5-speed or the 6L45/6L50 6-speed automatic. All LT-series vehicles, car or truck, use the 6LXX series of automatic transmission. These are very large transmissions and require extensive modification to the transmission tunnel and floorpan for use in GM A-Body platforms.

The aftermarket also offers custom-application GM transmissions that work great for LS swaps. The TCI 6X 6-speed automatic, for example, is based on the 4L80E with new guts, provides six forward gears, and is capable of handling 850 hp. The TCI 6X can be configured in several ways and comes with a TCI transmission controller. It can even be set up for paddle shift.

Manual Transmissions

The 6-speed T56 manual is the most popular transmission used in

LS engine swaps. Formerly offered on the 1998–2002 F-Body and GTO, the T56 bellhousing, flywheel, and clutch pack are readily available. The T56 transmission fits into most GM muscle cars, requiring only minor modifications to the transmission tunnel, if you set the engine forward 1.5 inches. When using the rear "stock" bellhousing position, extensive tunnel mods are required. Swap kits are available to help make the install easier. American Powertrain offers a complete T56 swap kit for GM A-Body platforms, simplifying the entire process.

The clutch mechanism, however, requires modifications. The hydraulic clutch is required for T56 swaps, and unless you use a kit such as the American Powertrain Hydramax system, it can become messy fast. You need a hydraulic release bearing and a clutch master cylinder, and then you need to adapt the pedal to the master. (See the special section "3- to 4-Speed Floor Shifter Conversion" for more information on the process.)

Performance Project: 3- to 4-Speed Floor Shifter Conversion

Dropping an LS or 4L60E transmission into your GM A-Body is a process of details. The physical installation is generally a simple task, but the details can cause major hassles. Wiring and plumbing details are manageable, but here is one you might not have thought about: connecting your 3-speed floor shifter to operate the 4-speed transmission. Unfortunately, it is not as simple as connecting the linkage. On GM A-Body cars, the floor shifter is designed specifically to shift 3-speeds; it does not function properly with 4-speeds.

The issue is the detent block. To keep the shifter locked into position, most A-Body floor shifters have a special detent block that is engaged by a locking post on the shifter arm. Some of these are "horseshoe" shifters with two vertical posts and a bridge handle; others have a single T-shape stalk and handle. Either way, both have push buttons that lock the shifter in Park and lock out Reverse.

Sure, you could junk the old stocker and drop in a new Hurst or B&M shifter, but that also requires replacing or modifying the factory console, which adds so much character to a bucket-seat A-Body. The best solution is to modify the shifter with a kit from Shiftworks. These kits range from as little as $30 (basic linkage kits for column shifters) up to $100 for the floor-shift models. Shiftworks has kits for all A-Body styles including one for 6LXX 6-speeds.

For the LT1-swapped 1971 Buick GS, I am using a 4L65E transmission. This kit bolts on in a matter of minutes and connects to the transmission with the factory cable using the new transmission pan-mount tab. The kit allows for adjustment of the linkage to ensure that the proper engagement is achieved as well. None of the modifications can be seen with the shifter installed; it looks completely factory.

The kit comes with a 4-speed decal, which works for a Chevelle but does not really match the style of the GS console. That is a minor issue and relatively easy to fix. I just left the console as is for the stock look. Shifting the transmission is just like factory; it has all the right detents and shift positions.

1 *The first step is to remove the shifter cable. There is a clip at the front of the shifter bracket. Pop this off.*

2 *The detent plate locks into the horizontal bar that is raised and lowered by the handle trigger. This is replaced.*

3 *Remove the pin that holds the shifter cable to the clevis.*

4 You can do all the work in the car, but this is a great time to inspect the shifter and replace any worn parts, so I pulled it from the car.

5 The detent unbolts from the shifter base. Two bolts hold it in place.

6 When you compare the detents, you can see the added shift points.

7 Load the new detent into the shifter, locking the detent bar into the Park position.

8 Bolt the detent plate into the shifter base.

9 Run the shifter through the gears, checking each detent. If your trigger springs are weak, you may want to replace them. Also check the bushings for fit; if they are loose, replace them. You can bolt the shifter back into the car now.

10 The kit comes with the new detent, a new cable support bracket, and a new adjustable shifter lever for the transmission. I replaced the shifter cable as well, but that is not required.

11 Under the car I installed the shifter lever to the 4L65E shifter pawl. Locate the adjustable clevis for the cable that bolts in the slot on the shift lever.

12 The cable bracket mounts to the transmission oil pan using the center two bolts. Secure the shift cable to this bracket.

13 The cable slides over the clevis. Set the shift positions to make sure the transmission is not overshifted.

The 1993–1997 T56s use an external clutch slave cylinder; later 1998–up units use an internal slave cylinder. The 1998–up T56 transmission is better suited for the Gen III/IV engines with the correct bolt pattern and input shaft, but McLeod offers components that adapt older T56 transmissions to the Gen III/IV engines.

Early T56 transmissions (1993–1999 LT1-compatible units) can be converted to mate to an LS or 2014–up Gen V LT-series engine with a different input shaft. The input shaft is quite simple to change (see the special section, "Fitting an Early T56 to an LS Engine" for more on the conversion).

Performance Project: Fitting an Early T56 to an LS Engine

More is usually better. More power, more torque, more, more, more. When it comes to transmissions, more gears are always better. The more gears you have, the faster you go while keeping your engine in the powerband. That is the key characteristic that made the Muncie M21 "Rockcrusher" transmission so popular. It was a close-ratio gearbox; each shift was a small jump, so you could keep the RPM up, with no big drop in engine speed to slow you down as you blasted down Main Street. Compared to a 3-speed, the 4s were always better. The ultimate in manual transmissions these days is the Tremec T56 6-speed.

Like the Muncies of the late 1960s, the T56 comes in a few flavors; be sure your version matches your needs. Originally designed for the Viper in 1992, the T56 has been a staple of high-performance American muscle for more than 20 years. Essentially, the T56 is a 4-speed with two overdrive gears. Fourth gear is always 1:1, while fifth is .84:1 down to 74:1, and sixth could be as low as .50:1, meaning your driveshaft is spinning twice as fast as your engine.

Input shafts vary in both length and girth (spline count). This is the most important spec because matching your engine to the transmission is tricky. The older LT (1990s GM) input shaft is shorter and uses a pusher-type throwout bearing. Most late-model engine swaps, including Gen III through Gen V GM engines, require the LS version of the input shaft.

I happened to have in the shop an LT1 T56 from a 1996 Camaro. To mate this bad boy to an LS, some modification is required. The LT version of the T56 is readily available in salvage yards for just a few hundred bucks, so I picked one up and got to work.

I sourced an LS input shaft, adapter plate, and a hydraulic clutch system from American Powertrain, and the new front bearing for the input shaft was ordered online. Swapping the input shaft is not complicated, but it is important to follow a few steps: Remove the cover and carefully pull out the input shaft. Press the new bearing onto the new shaft. When installing the shaft into the transmission, a slight rotation is needed to line up the gears. Then reinstall the cover.

The next part requires a dial indicator, a magnetic base, a piece of steel, and some clamps. Place the steel across the front cover, clamp it down, and lock the dial indicator to rest against the end of the input shaft. The factory spec is .0005 to .0035 inch. Push the input shaft in, zero the indicator, and then pull the shaft out. Note this number. The end play is adjustable through the shims behind the race in the front cover.

Once the end play is set, apply some assembly lube to the front bearing, install the front cover with a carefully placed thin bead of silicone, and torque to 26 ft/lbs. Too much silicone can gum up the internals of the transmission, so use just enough to seal the case.

With these steps handled, the T56 is ready for installation into any LS or 2014–up LT-series swap. Because the early versions of the T56 are so much cheaper than the newer LS version, it just makes sense.

1 *Begin by removing the bolts for the front cover. Keep these bolts, as they will be reused. Make sure you drain the transmission first.*

2 *Using a mallet, lightly tap the corners of the front cover to separate it from the case. It may be glued in place with silicone.*

3 *Carefully remove the input shaft assembly from the transmission. A slight twist walks the shaft out.*

4 *The LT1 (GM Gen II engine) shaft is on the left. The new LS-style shaft is on the right; notice that it is about 1 inch longer. The two are otherwise identical.*

5 *The Tremec T56s for the LT1 use a clutch fork with an external slave cylinder. The stub on the transmission has to go. I chopped it off with a cut-off wheel.*

7 You also need a new inner bearing race, which you also press into the back of the gear.

6 Using a hydraulic press and a length of thick-wall tubing, press the new bearing onto the new input shaft.

8 To set the end play, install the shaft and front cover and use a dial indicator to check the end play. The factory tolerance is .0005 to .0035 inch. Mine was loose, so it needs more shims.

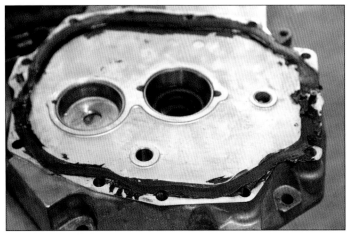

10 Seal the cover with silicone; you need only a thin layer. Too much can cause problems with the internals.

9 The shims do not come with the bearings, but I found some extra shims from a rear differential kit that fit just fine. I replaced the race with a new one and pressed it into the front cover.

11 *Before the final cover install, pre-lube the bearing with some assembly lube. Don't forget this step.*

12 *Make sure the guide pins line up with the case and then install the original bolts and torque them to 25 ft-lbs.*

Although the T56 has traditionally been the favored 6-speed manual gearbox, Tremec has replaced it with an updated version. Actually, the TR6060 and Super Magnum T56 are the two available versions. The Super Magnum T56 is the better option; it's available in the aftermarket and from Chevrolet Performance.

The Super Magnum T56 is one stout transmission that's capable of transmitting 700 ft-lbs of torque. The gearing is set at 2.66, 1.78, 1.3, 1.00, .80, and .63 dual overdrive. This will hit your wallet pretty hard at more than $4,500. It is, however, the strongest 6-speed manual.

The TR6060 is essentially an original T56 case with beefier internals. Those larger guts take up a lot of room. Because the case had to stay the same size, the extra room had to be taken from somewhere. The result leaves a little to be desired from the TR6060. Tremec's solution was to use smaller synchronizers. They are very fragile, and grinding the gears even once can wreck the synchro for that gear.

If the synchro is damaged, it will eventually fail and you will start burning up the gears themselves. Because of this, the TR6060 is not the best candidate for an LS swap. It will certainly function, but be aware that these transmissions are prone to failure. Should you choose to use a TR6060 in your swap, make sure you use Redline D4 ATF transmission fluid or Royal Purple SynchroMax. These oils have been reported to reduce cold-shift grinding and provide a better overall shifting feel for the TR6060.

When it comes to mounting the hydraulic clutch master cylinder, you can build a piecemeal kit yourself, fabricate the mount, or purchase a kit through American Powertrain, Detroit Speed, and others. The first component is the firewall master cylinder mount. Street & Performance offers brackets for use with a GM clutch master cylinder (GM PN 12570277) designed for GM cars 1958–1964 and separate parts for 1967–up models. Once the cylinder is in place, a line is run to the hydraulic clutch bearing. A fluid reservoir gets mounted on the firewall.

On the Chevelle build featured in this book, a hydraulic system from American Powertrain was used. This greatly simplified installation of the M21 Muncie 4-speed. The Hydramax hydraulic bearing uses a stack of shims to set the depth of the bearing. This allows for a perfect mesh for the clutch diaphragm. The hydraulics are relatively simple to install. The kit comes with a Wilwood master cylinder and can be bolted directly to the firewall where the stock pushrod comes through. The supplied bracket for the master cylinder is adjustable for angle.

An adapter tab may be required to bolt the original clutch pedal to the master cylinder pushrod. This tab must be fabricated and welded to the clutch pedal. The placement of this tab is critical. If the tab is too high, the pushrod does not fully engage. If

LS engines are designed to be used with a hydraulic-actuated clutch. You can make them work with manual clutches, but it takes a lot of effort. (Photo Courtesy Blane Burnett)

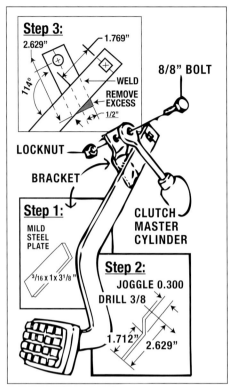

Step 3: 2.629" 1.769" 114° WELD REMOVE EXCESS 1/2" 8/8" BOLT

LOCKNUT BRACKET CLUTCH MASTER CYLINDER

Step 1: MILD STEEL PLATE 3/16 x 1 x 3 1/8"

Step 2: JOGGLE 0.300 DRILL 3/8 1.712" 2.629"

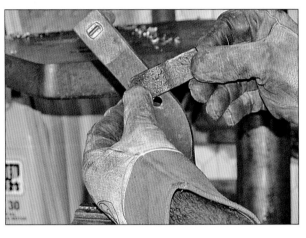

Place the tab into position just before welding. Be sure it remains correctly positioned according to the diagram. Keep in mind, this is only necessary when using a hydraulic clutch.

Converting to a hydraulic clutch requires modification of the stock clutch pedal. This diagram works for all GM muscle cars, including A-Bodies, but double check your application before welding anything.

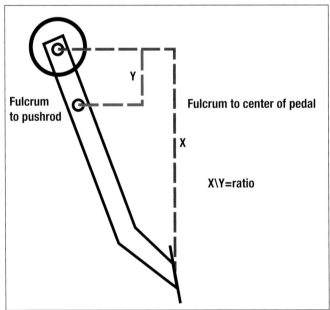

Y

Fulcrum to pushrod

Fulcrum to center of pedal

X

X\Y=ratio

This diagram shows the formula to calculate pedal ratio. Optimal pedal ratio for a hydraulic clutch is 7:1, but you can get away with 5:1 if necessary.

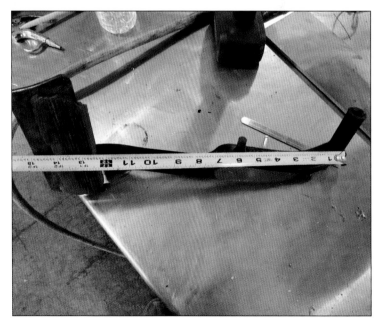

Take careful measurements on the pedal. You can get close with the pedal in the car, but it is much easier with the pedal on the workbench.

If you must move the pick-up point on the pedal, it is best to remove it from the car and drill it on the bench. A drill press is best, but if you don't have one, use a hand drill, starting with a small drill bit and working your way up.

it is placed too low, the pedal is hard to push.

Using a piece of 3/16-inch-thick mild plate steel cut to 1 x 3⅛ inches, the tab should be spaced .300 inch, starting at the 1.712-inch mark. Once bent, drill the tab with a 3/8-inch hole, measured from the long side of the tab at 2.629 inches on center. The placement of the tab on the pedal is 1.769 inches from the center of the square hole at the top of the pedal, and it sits at 114 degrees from the pedal side to the top of the tab. The tab should then be fully welded to the pedal arm. Trim off the small triangular-shaped section of the tab that overhangs the pedal on the underside. The clutch pushrod bolts to the tab via a 3/8-inch bolt and locknut.

Using the stock pushrod linkage hole increases the pedal effort on the clutch. By raising the pick-up point on the pedal, the effort needed to disengage the clutch is greatly reduced. This pedal ratio is the difference in length between the pivot (fulcrum) of the pedal to the pushrod hole (Y) and the fulcrum to the center of the brake pedal (X). A hydraulic master system should be between 5:1 and 7:1.

Consider this: A master cylinder with a 1-inch bore and a pedal ratio of 6:1 with 100 pounds of pedal pressure yields 600 pounds of pressure at the master cylinder. Reduce the pedal ratio to 4:1 and the pressure at the master drops to just 400 pounds. That is a significant difference and increases your effort by 33 percent. You can use the stock hole in the stock A-Body pedals, but it absolutely will be more difficult to operate.

It is possible to adapt an LS engine to use a manual clutch linkage. If you are installing an LS and manual transmission in a GM vehicle originally available with a manual clutch setup, you need linkage, clutch, Z-bar, and related components. The Gen III/IV blocks are not drilled for the Z-bar, which makes it difficult to adapt the LS engine to a manual linkage. Fabricating a simple bracket that locates off the bellhousing bolts and attaches to the Z-bar is the best solution.

The T56 has a top-mounted shifter at the rear of the transmission that creates a small compatibility issue for the stock console or shifter location in GM vehicles. An S&P shifter relocator kit easily resolves the problem. This piece from Driveline Components is built for your specific placement needs. Because engine and transmission mounts differ, each shifter must be ordered individually. The T56 relocator shifter can move the shifter 1 to 4.1 inches forward. In addition, the shifter can be centered or offset to the left or right. If you choose to use the stock T56 shifter, place it 4 to 5 inches rearward from the stock location. The Viper T56 uses the forward-mounted shifter position, but this requires adapter plates for LS swaps.

Another popular manual swap is the Tremec TKO 500 or TKO 600. These 5-speed manual transmissions are very popular among GM muscle builders and offer excellent performance. American Powertrain offers complete kits for installing the TKO (and T56) for the GM A-Body platform. These kits feature hydraulic clutches, bellhousing, and all the components to make the installation simple and easy. TKO transmissions use a top-mounted shifter as well. To adapt these shifters to the stock location, a Hurst Blackjack shifter can reposition the shifter to the ideal location.

The TKO transmission does not fit quite as neatly under the body as the T56 does. The transmission fits some GM vehicles without modification, but the 1964–1972 GM A-Body platform requires a large section of the transmission tunnel be removed and replaced with a reshaped panel. The American Powertrain kits come with the requisite patch panel, cut

If the car did not have a manual transmission before, you can simply cut the hole in the ideal location.

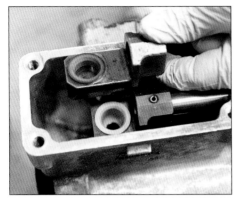

The shifters are interchangeable as long as you swap the receiver bolted inside the transmission.

This shows the difference between the GTO shifter (left) and a new Hurst F-Body-style shifter (right). The placement of the handle is everything in the type of shifter you use. The Hurst shifter is also more accurate through precision machining. (Photo Courtesy Blane Burnett)

If your car has a manual transmission and you want to retain the stock console, you need an adjustable shifter, such as this one from Driveline Components Company. This shifter allows for clearance of some floorpans.

When mating an LS to an older manual transmission, it is difficult to make the manual clutch system work. Here is the truck-style bellhousing with mid-length headers on a Vortec 5.3. The exhaust is clearly in the way of the clutch fork and pivot ball.

The stock truck-style manifolds are also in the way of the Z-bar and the pushrod hits the manifold down low. A hydraulic system is the best solution.

guide, and instructions, taking the guesswork out of the swap.

For varying reasons, from nostalgia to economy to personal taste to simplicity to originality, some builders prefer to keep the stock manual gearbox in their muscle car or truck when swapping in a Gen III/IV engine. These swaps bolt up like automatic transmissions do, but require a few specialized pieces.

The input shaft is too far from the crank with a stock bellhousing, the same situation as with a manual transmission. You have two ways to remedy this problem. The first and best way is to use a retrofit bellhousing and flywheel package. General Motors sells these components individually through its Chevy Performance dealers such as Pace Performance.

The Chevy Performance retrofit bellhousing features thick-wall titanium-aluminum alloy construction, CNC machining including spot-faced mounting holes, precision dowel pin holes, and bores that yield a precise fit. This bellhousing bolts to all GM Gen III/IV V-8 engines for installation of the Muncie, T-10, Saginaw, Richmond, Tremec TKO, Tremec T56-011, and other specially built transmissions. This bellhousing works with stock clutch linkage and hydraulic clutch actuators. It includes a steel inspection cover and mounting hardware, and it's designed to use a 168-tooth flywheel and standard GM starter. This bellhousing is lightweight at only 15 pounds, and uses all factory linkage parts, including clutch forks, Z-bar, rubber dust boot, etc. According to Chevy Performance, you must use the LS truck flywheel (PN 12561680), a 12-inch clutch and pressure plate (PN RAM88744), and six metric pressure plate bolts (PN 12561465).

You can also use an original Chevy big-block manual transmission bellhousing instead of buying a new one. The specific part you need is the 621 Chevy big-block bellhousing. This fits the Chevelle chassis and the LS engine without issue. The Chevy small-block and truck bellhousings have clearance issues. The flywheel needs to fit the LS and have a standard Chevy small-block clutch bolt pattern. I used a PRW conversion flywheel (PN 1634680) on the 1969 Chevelle shown in this book. For the pilot bearing, the LS7 bearing (PN 12557583) fits the LS flywheel and costs less than the extended conversion bearings and works just as well.

Adapting an early manual transmission to an LS takes a bit of forethought and a few special parts. This is the LS7 pilot bearing, an off-the-shelf part that drops right into the 5.3's crank.

This bearing is a press fit, so you can use a large socket or bearing driver to tap it into the crank.

Coat the flywheel bolts with medium threadlocker and thread them into the crank. LS crank bolts are torque-to-yield; you must replace them with ARP standard flywheel bolts or with new GM torque-to-yield bolts.

Install the flywheel and torque to spec. The specs depend on the bolts you are using, so check with the manufacturer of the bolts; the standard for LS engines is 74 ft-lbs. This PRW flywheel has a dual-clutch pattern for LS and Gen I Chevy small-block engines.

Make sure you mount the clutch with the correct side to the flywheel; look for the sticker or engraving. This is a 10-spline clutch for a Chevy small-block Gen I engine.

Use the alignment tool to lock the clutch in place with the pilot bearing. This Advanced Clutch Technology heavy-duty steel spring clutch is capable of handling 735 ft-lbs of torque, which makes it about perfect for the stock 5.3 Vortec with room for eventual performance upgrades.

Install the diaphragm to the flywheel. There are multiple bolt patterns on the flywheel; find the right holes and line it up.

Use a couple of bolts to secure the bellhousing and then a straightedge or caliper to measure the depth of the transmission mounting pad to the diaphragm fingers. Measure in three places and note each measurement. Take the average of these to use as measurement A.

The hydraulic release bearing mounts on a stud in the transmission. The American Powertrain kit comes with several studs to match the threads from the front bearing cover. Remove one bolt and match the threads.

Install the stud into the transmission and be sure to use medium threadlocker on the threads. Then bend the retaining tabs back over the hex on the stud.

The Hydramax bearing slides over the input shaft and locks in place on the stud. This is a free-floating unit; it does not get bolted down.

Measure the distance between the release bearing and the transmission mounting flange. Make sure that you measure from the top of the bearing. This is measurement B.

Use this formula to determine the number of shims required: (A − B) -.150 inch ÷ .90 (width of a GM shim). For example, 2.45 - 2.125 - .150 ÷ .90 = 1.9 shims, so you round it up and use two shims. You can run as little gap as .100 inch, but .150 to .200 is optimum. Stack up the shims and install them behind the bearing.

Remove the bellhousing from the engine and bolt it to the transmission using new Grade-8 bolts.

Each hydraulic line threads onto the bearing and runs out of the bellhousing through the clutch fork hole. Secure the lines with a wire clamp.

Now the engine and transmission are mated together and ready for installation in the vehicle.

The clutch depends on the transmission you are using. There are 10- and 26-spline input shafts. Make sure you have the right clutch for your transmission; beyond that, any Chevy small-block clutch works, provided your flywheel has the Chevy small-block clutch pattern. A 26-spline transmission can use a stock truck LS manual flywheel with a matching LS clutch.

If you use the conversion flywheel, the stock- length (1.25 inches) throwout bearing works great. For stock flywheel and clutch combinations, an extended throwout bearing is required. General Motors offers a 1.75-inch-length bearing (PN PT614037) for these applications. This requires using the stock mechanical pushrod clutch linkage.

Aftermarket versions of these parts in complete kit form are available from sources such as McLeod and Advance Adapters. These clutch kits are designed to adapt the Gen III/IV engines to early-style GM manual transmissions such as the M21/M22, SM420, SM465, and NV4500. Also, these kits allow the installation of Richmond Gear manual transmissions such as the ROD 6-speed. The Advance Adapter clutch kits typically include a custom flywheel, 11-mm flywheel bolts, 11-inch Centerforce pressure plate and disc, pilot bushing spacer, throwout bearing, collector gasket, 10-mm bellhousing bolts, 10-mm lock washers, and XRP dowel bolts.

If you want to assemble your own parts kit, you need to match the flywheel and clutch to the output of the engine and make sure the splines on the clutch disc match the transmission. GM transmissions use 10- and 26-spline input shafts, the early manuals (before 1971) typically have 10 splines, and the later units have 26 splines. That said, other aftermarket manual transmissions have either 10 or 26 splines. The 26-spline shaft is more durable than a 10-spline shaft because it distributes the input load better.

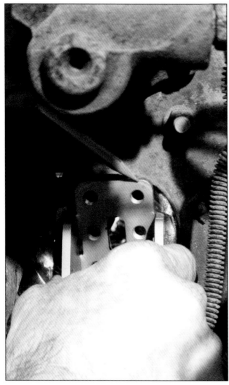

In the engine bay, the clutch master cylinder mounts to the firewall. You can use the stock clutch rod location with a slight modification. The adjustable bracket that comes with the Hydramax kit needs a little trimming to clear the opening in the firewall. I marked it with a pencil.

I used a sander to remove the offending material. It doesn't take much to get the universal bracket to fit.

I also marked the factory plate that bolts to the firewall for the bracket. Four holes needed to be drilled out to establish a slot for the pushrod as well.

With these mods, the master cylinder bolts to the fire-wall and clears the brakes and steering column; it also clears in power-brake cars. The reservoir will be remote-mounted.

Under the dash, I measured for the pedal pushrod. The kit comes with a length of rod, a coupler, and a rod end. Measure twice, cut once, and leave a little extra for adjustment.

The linkage rod bolts in and fits quite well. I did not have to modify the pedal ratio, but the pedal is a little stiffer than the stock manual linkage. That can be adjusted later if necessary.

The remote reservoir mounts next to the hood hinge at the top. The key to locating the reservoir is to make sure it is above the master cylinder with access to fill it.

Torque Capacity Formula

For a clutch to do its job it must perform well in these three areas: clamp load, friction coefficient, and surface area. These determine the torque capacity. The formula for calculating this is as follows:

$$T = P \times F \times N \times R$$

Where:

T = Torque at the flywheel
P = Clamping force (a function of the diaphragm)
F = Friction coefficient
N = Friction surface quantity
R = Radius of the friction surface

The braided line goes to the bearing and the rubber line goes to the reservoir. The kit comes with a press-on cap for the master cylinder–to-reservoir line.

The other option is to use an extended bearing, so you can use the original old-style bellhousing. Match the clutch to the engine and use a longer bearing to make up the difference for the shorter crank flange. Several manufacturers offer extended bearings including McLeod, PN 8617, and GM, PN 12557583. By using the old-style bellhousing, you should have a provision for the Z-bar and be able to run a manual clutch set-up.

Clutch Basics

A typical manual-shift car almost always comes with the standard, basic single-disc clutch from the factory. They are durable, have a good pedal feel, and work great for low to medium performance. The clutch's job is to transfer the power of the engine to the transmission and to sever that link when required. That doesn't sound like much, but considering the massive power output we are seeing on the street, holding that connection without slipping is a tough job. The two main types of clutch are: disc-sprung hub and solid hub.

Most street clutches have a sprung hub. A set of six to eight springs absorb a small amount of the impact from the spinning flywheel as it grabs the stationary clutch, and it reduces the chatter and noise from the clutch. In addition, clutches have a set of limit pins; think of them as bumpstops that set the maximum rotational limits for the hub-to-disc connection. If your hub springs are too light, the engine bounces off the limit pins, which results in chatter.

The Marcel spring is a device often used in clutch discs; it reduces chatter as well. Thin washer-type springs sit between the disc and the clutch facing.

Solid hubs are more race oriented; they do not chatter and help enable smooth shifting. Solid-hub clutches do not last long on the street due to the vibrational fatigue on the splines.

The torque capacity can be determined using simple multiplication. For example, if you have 650 ft-lbs of torque as a maximum flywheel load, you can work backward using known variables. The coefficient of friction is one of the items that you might find listed in the specifications table for a clutch. Rough numbers are .25 for organic, .36 for ceramic, and .40 for sintered iron. These general guideline numbers are not product specific, but a good place to start. As a rule, the higher the coefficient number, the better the grip at a cost of wear life and chatter.

Disc Options

The number of friction surfaces is the same as the number of clutch sides. A single disc has two friction surfaces; a dual disc has four. The size of the clutch disc determines the radius. Clamping force is determined by the pressure plate and how the springs leverage the disc. Increasing the fulcrum length does not affect the pedal pressure, but the spring force does. However, increasing the fulcrum length does reduce the life of the clutch.

Many compromises must be made in clutch system design because

A complete kit, such as this one from ACT, includes a matched flywheel. This ensures everything is balanced and functions properly together. The ACT single-disc clutch transmits 770 ft-lbs with a sintered metallic clutch disc. (Photo Courtesy ACT)

certain changes affect the holding power. Increasing the spring rate of the pressure plate increases clamping force, which also increases pedal effort, especially with a nonhydraulic pedal. You can increase the diameter of the clutch; this also means you need a larger flywheel, which soaks up more power and slows the rev time. Clutch design is a fine balance of criteria.

Adding a second disc to the clutch pack significantly increases the torque capacity. Dual-disc clutches don't require high static clamp pressures, so the lighter pedal requires less effort to engage and disengage. A dual-disc clutch has double the friction surface, so they can use organic friction materials, which provide a smoother engagement (less chatter) and longer life. This is the reason dual-disc design has become so popular in street and street/strip

applications. Although a single-disc system may transmit 600 ft-lbs, a similar dual-disc system can hold 1,200 with less pedal pressure.

Two types of twin-disc systems are available: strap driven and stand driven. The distinction refers to the style in which the center floating plate is driven. Strap-driven floater plates are attached to the flywheel with a set of straps. This adds a little weight to the flywheel, but it makes for very quiet operation. Most street applications are better off with a strap-driven floater.

The stand-driven floater plates float between a set of posts between the pressure plate and the flywheel. When idling, the floater tends to rattle, which could be annoying in a street car. The stand-driven unit allows for faster shifting, which is good for completion.

Multi-disc clutches do come

with a few drawbacks. The distance between the flywheel and the transmission is a finite area, so there is limited space for adding clutch discs. This can be an issue with some factory hydraulic slave cylinders as they have a limited length of travel. The disc height must be tuned to the car as well, so you want a multi-disc kit that has everything, including the flywheel. Otherwise you will be learning how to set disc height.

Pressure Plates

The clutch does the hard work; the pressure plate is the mechanism that releases and engages the disc. The three types of pressure plates are: diaphragm, long, and Borg & Beck. Each design has benefits in their useful areas.

Diaphragm pressure plates are the most common in street applications. This is what you think of when someone says "pressure plate"; the diaphragm is a series of long spring bars that fan out around the release bearing. These are effective for street and high-performance street applications because they have excellent spring pressures, load the clutch disc evenly throughout the entire diameter, and have a break-over point. This means that the clutch pressure reduces significantly at the point where the springs are over center. When you are stuck at a traffic light, your thigh will thank you.

Long-style plates are more often seen in strictly drag racing applications. The Long style uses three narrow fingers that couple the release bearing to a group of nine springs around the pressure plate. To release the clutch, the nine springs must be compressed. This design is very popular for the quick shifts of drag racing. The long style is very tunable through spring rates, stand height, and centrifugal weights. The centrifugal weights add additional force on the clutch because the engine spins faster.

Borg & Beck is a version of the long style that uses three fingers to compress springs for disc release. This style uses rollers that swing out as the engine revs to increase disc pressure. McLeod's version provides consistent action for fast shifting.

Friction Material

The friction material is just as important as the rest of the design. Organic, Kevlar/carbon, ceramic, and metallic are the four types of friction materials used in clutches, with countless variations including hybrids. As discussed earlier, the higher the friction coefficient, the more grab the material has at a cost of wear life. Other factors to consider when choosing friction material include engagement, holding power, and glaze resistance.

Organic friction materials consist of metal fibers woven into an organic fiber, the most common being fiberglass, carbon fiber, brass wire, and a few proprietary binders to keep it all together. The binding resins create some durability and performance problems with organic clutches. As with brake pads, overheating causes them to glaze. That nose-hair singeing smell you get when you roast the clutch (or brake pads) is the resin burning. When it cools, both surfaces are left with a thin layer of slippery crystallized resin. Although organic clutches are susceptible to overheating, they are very capable for most street cars. Organic materials are the softest of all the friction materials, which means low chatter, smooth engagement, and good holding power.

Kevlar/carbon discs are a good alternative to organic clutches on street/strip cars. Made in a similar manner to organics, the Kevlar fibers are weaved and compressed with a resin. They are harder than organics, so they chatter more. One of the issues with these types of clutches is that although they have excellent heat resistance in the clutch, they also retain heat. That means that the flywheel becomes hotter and stays hot. Once you overheat a Kevlar clutch, it does not recover quickly. These materials are excellent for street/strip applications that don't see a lot of stop-and-go traffic.

Ceramic clutches are very good at absorbing heat and wicking it away from the mating surfaces of the pressure plate and flywheel. They have better holding power than organic materials. Ceramic materials suffer, however, in durability and chatter. The hardness of the materials makes them chatter much more than organics with their abrupt engagement. This also wears out the mating surfaces faster than with organics. Ceramics wear faster than Kelvar/carbon clutches, but have higher heat tolerance. Stop-and-go traffic can be an issue for ceramic clutches.

Metallic clutches are made of sintered iron and sometimes bronze; they are extremely hard. The sintering process heats the particles to red hot and then compresses them together, leaving a rough block. Although not quite melted, they are heated to the point that they stick together, so there is no resin to overheat and glaze. These bad boys chatter a lot, but they also have the highest holding power. They are not street friendly because the engagement is very abrupt. This means they wear out the mating surfaces quickly. Metallic clutches are capable of handling more than 750 hp in a single-disc system.

Hybrid clutches use one material type on one side and a different material on the other. This allows the clutch maker to blend characteristics of both materials. For example, a McLeod 500 clutch has organic pads on the flywheel side with segmented ceramic on the pressure plate side. This provides longer wear life for the flywheel and smoother engagement but better hold through the pressure plate.

WIRING HARNESSES AND WIRING

Integrating the LS engine wiring harness into an A-Body wiring harness requires careful planning, a solid understanding of automotive electrical wiring, and patience to complete the complex work. Undoubtedly, this is one of the most challenging aspects of a swap project.

Most builders are familiar with fabrication techniques, trouble shooting, and parts swapping to make things work, but electronics rise to a much higher level of complexity. Wiring comes with an aura of mystery that can send a shiver down the spine of even the most seasoned builders, making them wish for a simple carburetor and distributor. If you fall into this group, don't lose hope. This book has the answers you seek with easy-to-understand instructions for tackling the wiring of an LS swap into an A-Body.

Gen III/IV engines feature complex computers that control everything from timing and ignition to fuel and air intake. On many LS engines, even the throttle is computer controlled; the pedal is connected to a sensor box that tells the throttle how far to open. These systems can be overwhelming, but the key is to break it down and take it one circuit at a time. Although the factory systems are certainly adequate, the

Chevrolet Performance wiring harnesses have only the wires you need for swap installs. Similar to aftermarket offerings, these are plug-and-play harnesses, and only a few wires need to be terminated and connected.

You can use a stock harness in your swap as is, or give it the "wire diet" by cutting off the loom and removing wires that are not needed. This is a great way to get to know your engine's wiring in detail. Keeping track of each wire can be a bit of a headache, though.

You cannot rush a wiring harness install. Whether you use a stock or aftermarket harness, you need professional caliber connectors so the electrical system and all electronics perform their best. With this project, I installed Painless Performance PowerBraid to protect the wires from abrasions and heat while keeping a stock look.

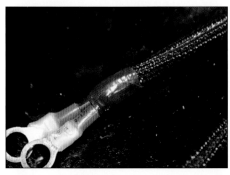

Friction tape on the ends secures the braid. You can use regular electrical tape, but make sure it is high quality, such as 3M Super 33.

This is a completed wire-diet LS1 harness install with the full loom. This takes some time to complete, but the results are worth it.

acquire all of them with the engine. Matching key components, such as a TAC module, with the ECM can be difficult without all vehicle/engine specific details such as year, make, and model. If you already have the engine, but it did not come with any of the extras, that is okay; you can mix and match ECMs and engines, but the ECM must match the wiring harness.

Cam Sensor Locations

Two locations are available for the cam sensor on LS engines. Gen III engines use a rear-mounted cam sensor on the back of the block, behind the intake. A long cam sensor reads the back of the camshaft. Later-model Gen IV engines use a different cam sensor mounted in the timing cover that reads the cam position off the timing gear. The placement is interchangeable, but you need the correct cam and gear for your ECM.

Retrofitting the stock wiring harness may seem complex and perhaps overwhelming, but it really is not that difficult. With the proper diagrams and instructions, the stock wiring harness can be modified to greatly simplify the process of wiring the engine. Most of the wires in the stock harness are not needed in a retrofit application.

The following is a basic guideline for an LS1 stock retrofit wiring harness. There are more ways to skin this cat; this is just one of them. This pin-out guide is from a 1999 LS1.

The 1997–1998 LS1 wiring harness is different from the one used on 1999–2002 models, and the Vortec truck harnesses are different from that. These guidelines do not include wiring for AIR injection, A/C, traction control, or cruise control.

aftermarket has fully embraced the LS platform and there is more than one way to do it right.

Take-Out Harnesses

If you are working on a budget swap, you likely have bought a "take-out" engine. The key to keeping the swap under budget is to use as many factory components as possible, and the wiring harness is absolutely part of that equation. When you source a salvage engine,

you need all the electrical components that go with it. Let me repeat that: It is imperative to have everything, and this includes the computer, wiring harness, MAF sensor, oxygen sensors, and if the engine is DBW, the gas pedal and TAC module.

Each engine requires the use of its own specific computer and harness, and keep in mind that there were changes made to each system year by year. To reuse as many of the factory components as possible, you need to

Crimp connectors are sufficient for most connections, but soldered connectors provide better conductivity with less voltage loss for the most important engine management systems. Most people do not properly fasten the crimp connectors. You want to start out by crossing the wires to be soldered and then wrapping the wires around each other (shown). You do not want a "pig tail"; the joint should resemble a single length of continuous wire. Next you heat the wires from the bottom of the joint, and apply the solder from the top. This draws the solder through the wire, yielding a proper connection and not a cold solder joint. You should be able to see individual strands of wire through the solder. If you can't, either you have too much solder or the wire wasn't hot enough.

Cover the connection with either shrink tubing or electrical tape. Tubing is better, but you must slide it over the wires (past the joint) before soldering.

Other components used in Gen III/IV wiring are Weather Pack and Metri-Pack terminals. These terminals contain small pins that require special tools to crimp. These are used in every connector on a late-model engine. Although most builders won't have disassemble and reassembling terminals, if you are retrofitting a stock harness, do this. These crimpers are available in many configurations and most have ratcheting locks that ensure a completed crimp.

Metri or Weather Pack terminals have a molex or nylon housing and a silicone wire seal around the terminals so the connections are solid, reliable, and will perform for years to come.

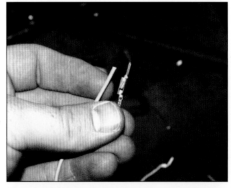

The terminals must be crimped twice: once on the bare wire and once on the silicone insulation. Make sure you slide the wire through the silicone boot before crimping.

Each terminal style has different pin types. All styles lock into the plug housing with spring locks built into the terminal itself. Unlocking these can be a pain; the trick is to use a small pick or unfolded paperclip to unlock it. Every terminal uses a different lock location.

Connectors for 1997–1998 LS1 Engines

Connector C100

Connector	Description
A	This is the power for the odd fuel injectors; route it to IGN 1 15A fuse
B	Not used.
C	Not used.
D	Not used.
E	Not used.
F	Not used.
G	Engine control power; route to IGN 3 15A fuse
H	Cooling fan 2/high-speed relay; route to terminal 86 of cooling fan 2 relay
J	Cooling fan 1/low-speed relay; route to terminal 86 of cooling fan 1 relay
K	Not used.

Connector C101

Connector	Description
A	Not used.
B	Power for even coils; route to IGN 2 15A fuse
C	Not used.
D	Output for fuel pump relay; route to terminal 85 of fuel pump relay
E	Computer power; route to IGN 4 15A fuse
F	Not used.
G	Constant computer power; route to BAT 1 10A fuse
H	Not used.
J	Not used.
K	Not used.

Connector C105

Connector	Description
A	Not used.
B	Engine sensor power; route to IGN 5 20A fuse
C	Not used.
D	Not used.
E	Serial data signal; route into car to Data Link Connector terminal 9 (or OBDII port)
F	Not used.
G	Not used.
H	Not used.

Connector C220

Connector	Description
A	Generator warning light negative (-) side. If your vehicle already has a GEN light, it should plug in and work. If your vehicle has an internal regulated alternator, connect this to the wire that connects to terminal 1 on the alternator. If you need to add a GEN light, wire this to one side of the light's terminals and the other side of the light's terminals to an ignition 12-volt fuse. The same wire with a 20-amp fuse can power all of the warning lights.
B	Oil pressure output. If using an LS1 oil-pressure sender with the stock gauge, connect this wire to the oil pressure gauge. The most common procedure is to use an aftermarket oil pressure-sending unit and delete this wire. The same wire with a 20-amp fuse can power all of the warning lights.
C	Low oil level warning lamp (- output, this is a negative trigger). This is also an optional accessory. If you want a low oil light, attach this wire to one terminal of a light and the other to a 12-volt ignition source (fused of course). The same wire with a 20-amp fuse can power all of the warning lights.
D	Not used.
E	Not used.
F	Not used.
G	Vehicle Speed Sensor (VSS) output from computer; this is a 4,000 pulse-per-mile square-wave output; it works for GM electronic speedometers as well as some aftermarket speedometers.
H	Not needed.
J	Not needed.
K	Temperature gauge output. This signal may work with older GM electronic temperature gauges, but it might not be as accurate. Most builders opt to install an aftermarket sending unit on the back of the block.

Connector C 230

Connector	Description
A	Not used.
B	This is the fabled "Service Engine Soon" light; it is a negative trigger output. Route this wire to one terminal of a 12-volt light bulb and the other terminal of the bulb to an ignition 12-volt fuse. The same wire with a 20-amp fuse can power all of the warning lights.
C	Not used.
D	Tachometer output. This is a 4-cylinder, two-pulse-per-revolution output. The tach must be able to be set to 4-cylinder or be a compatible GM tachometer.
E	VATS fuel enable. This wire is not needed if VATS has been deleted in the computer, or it could be retained and a VATS bypass box added for extra security. Most builders remove the VATS system because it is not very user friendly.
F	Not used.
G	Not used.
H	To brake torque converter clutch switch. A switch that provides 12 volts to this wire must be provided when the car is running. It cuts power when you press the brake pedal. There may be a cruise-control switch that does this already, or one may have to be added. Adding a microswitch (similar to those used in nitrous kits) from any electronics parts store works. Build a small bracket to hold the switch behind the brake pedal lever so the switch is depressed when the pedal is at rest but opens when the brake pedal is pushed down. One terminal needs to be connected to 12 volts ignition power, and the other to this wire. This is only for automatic transmission cars.
J	Park neutral position switch. This is a negative trigger output. If this switch is not wired, the car is able to be started in gear, which is bad. The stock shifter may have this already. If not, one needs to be added. The process is the same as for the brake converter switch (above). The terminals are wired to ground instead of power. This is only for automatic transmission cars.
K	Serial data output to the DLC or OBDII connector terminal 2. This is for an OBDII port for engine diagnostics and tuning.

Relays for 1997–1998 LS1 Engines

Based on the use of 30-amp Bosch-style automotive relays, relays 1, 2, and 3 can be combined into one if you use one 80-amp relay. Keeping them separate simplifies any troubleshooting; 80-amp relays cost quite a bit.

Relay 1

Terminal	Description
85	To conversion car wiring (a wire that is hot in run and start modes). This wire is typically used to power the original coil. The ballast resistor must be removed.
86	To ground.
30	Direct to battery voltage.
87	To 2 15A fuses (IGN 1 and IGN 2) IGN 1 fuse to pin A of C100 connector, and IGN 2 fuse to pin B of C101 connector.

Relay 2

Terminal	Description
85	To conversion car wiring (a wire that is hot in run and start modes). This wire typically powers the original coil. The ballast resistor must be removed.
86	To ground.
30	Direct to battery voltage.
87	To 2 15A fuses (IGN 3 and IGN 4) IGN 3 fuse to pin G of C100 connector, and IGN 4 fuse to pin E of C101 connector.

Relay 3

Terminal	Description
85	To conversion car wiring (a wire that is hot in run and start modes). This wire is typically used to power the original coil. The ballast resistor must be removed.
86	To ground.
30	Direct to battery voltage.
87	To 1 20A fuse (IGN 5), IGN 5 to pin B of connector C105.

Relay 4 Fuel Pump Relay

Terminal	Description
85	To pin D of connector C101.
86	To ground.
30	Direct to battery voltage.
87	To 1 20A fuse then to the fuel pump.

Cooling fans can use two relays or one, depending on the radiator fan setup. Two fans can be on one circuit that run at the same time, or the two fans can be wired to separate circuits, as with the factory version. One fan functions as a low-speed fan; the other is a high-speed fan, which comes on in the event the engine is not cooling down. Use the low-speed fan relay if running only one fan.

Relay 5 Cooling Fan 1/Slow Speed Fan

Terminal	Description
85	To conversion car wiring (a wire that is hot in run and start modes). This wire is typically used to power the original coil. The ballast resistor must be removed.
86	To pin J of connector C100.
30	Direct to battery voltage.
87	To a 20A fuse or larger, depending on cooling fan requirements.

Relay 6 Cooling Fan 2/High-Speed Fan

Terminal	Description
85	To conversion car wiring (a wire that is hot in run and start modes). This wire is typically used to power the original coil. The ballast resistor must be removed.
86	To pin H of C100 connector.
30	Direct to battery voltage.
87	To a 20A fuse or larger, depending on cooling fan requirements.

The last wire to connect is the starter wire. If the conversion car is a GM model, this is a large purple wire. Simply route it to the starter solenoid.

Connectors for 1999–2002 LS1 Engines

The later 1999–2002 LS1 wiring harnesses are different because the connections are different and there are more circuits. The following is a basic guide to a later LS1 retrofit harness. Most of the wires are the same, though the placement might be different. This does not include wiring for traction control, cruise, or A/C.

Connector C100

Connector	Description
A	This is the power for the odd fuel injectors; route to IGN 1 15A fuse.
B	Not used.
C	Not used.
D	Not used.
E	Not used.
F	Not used.
G	Engine control power, route to IGN 3 15A fuse.
H	Cooling fan 2/high-speed relay, route to terminal 86 of cooling fan 2 relay.
J	Cooling fan 1/low-speed relay, route to terminal 86 of cooling fan 1 relay.
K	Not used.

Connector C101

Connector	Description
A	Not used.
B	Power for even coils; route to IGN 2 15A fuse.
C	Not used.
D	Output for fuel pump relay; route to terminal 85 of fuel pump relay.
E	Computer power; route to IGN 4 15A fuse.
F	Not used.
G	Constant computer power; route to BAT 1 10A fuse.
H	Ground this wire.
J	Not used.
K	Not used.

Connector C105

Connector	Description
A	Not used.
B	Engine sensor power; route to IGN 5 20A fuse.
C	Not used.
D	Not used.
E	Not used.
F	Not used.
G	Tachometer output. This signal is a 4-cylinder, two pulse-per-revolution output. The tach must be able to be set on 4-cylinder or be a compatible GM electronic tachometer.
H	Not used on a 1999. For a 2002 harness, this is the EGR valve. EGR is typically bypassed for conversions.

Connector C220

Connector	Description
A	Oil pressure output. This signal can be used for a GM electronic oil-pressure gauge. If it does not work, install an aftermarket sending unit.
B	Clutch pedal position switch on a 6-speed transmission. This is obviously not used on an automatic.
C	Power supply to TCC stop lamp switch. This is not used in a 6-speed car or if the car already has a TCC stop switch. If the car does not have a stop lamp switch, use this to feed power to the switch.
D	To brake torque converter clutch switch. There must be a switch that provides 12 volts to this wire when the car is running and then cuts power when the brake pedal is depressed. There may be a cruise-control switch that does this already, or one may have to be added. Adding a microswitch (such as those used in nitrous kits) from any electronics parts store works. Build a small bracket to hold the switch behind the brake pedal lever so the switch is depressed when the pedal is at rest but opens when the brake pedal is pushed down. One terminal needs to be connected to 12-volt ignition power, and the other to this wire. This is only for automatic transmissions
E	This wire must be grounded.
F	Not used.
G	Reverse light switch for 6-speed transmissions. Not used in an automobile.
H	Park neutral position switch. This is a negative trigger output. If this switch is not wired, the car can be started in gear, which is bad. The stock shifter may have this already. If not, one needs to be added. The process is the same as for the brake converter switch (above). The terminals are wired to ground instead of power. This is only for automatic transmission cars.
J	Not used.
K	Vehicle Speed Sensor (VSS) output from computer. This is a 4,000 pulse-per-mile square wave output; it works for GM electronic speedometers, as well as some aftermarket speedometers.

Connector C 230

Connector	Description
A	Not used.
B	This is the fabled "Service Engine Soon" light. This is a negative trigger output. Route this wire to one terminal of a 12-volt light bulb and the other terminal of the bulb to an ignition 12-volt fuse. The same wire with a 20-amp fuse can power all of the warning lights.
C	Not used.

D	Not used.
E	VATS fuel enable. This wire is not needed if VATS has been deleted in the computer, or it could be retained and a VATS bypass box added for extra security, but the best way is to delete VATS altogether.
F	Not used.
G	Not used.
H	Not used.
J	Not used.
K	Serial data output to DLC or OBDII connector terminal 2.

Relays for 1999–2002 LS1 Engines

Based on the use of 30-amp Bosch-style automotive relays, relays 1, 2, and 3 can be combined into one with an 80-amp relay. However, keeping them separate simplifies any troubleshooting; 80-amp relays cost quite a bit.

Relay 1

Terminal	Description
85	To conversion car wiring (a wire that is hot in run and start modes). This wire is typically used to power the original coil. The ballast resistor must be removed.
86	To ground.
30	Direct to battery voltage.
87	To 2 15A fuses (IGN 1 and IGN 2) IGN 1 fuse to pin A of C100 connector, and IGN 2 fuse to pin B of C101 connector.

Relay 2

Terminal	Description
85	To conversion car wiring (a wire that is hot in run and start modes). This wire is typically used to power the original coil. The ballast resistor must be removed.
86	To ground.
30	Direct to battery voltage.
87	To 2 15A fuses (IGN 3 and IGN 4) IGN 3 fuse to pin G of C100 connector, and IGN 4 fuse to pin E of C101 connector.

Relay 3

Terminal	Description
85	To conversion car wiring (a wire that is hot in run and start modes). This wire is typically used to power the original coil. The ballast resistor must be removed.
86	To ground.
30	Direct to battery voltage.
87	To 1 20A fuse (IGN 5), IGN 5 to pin B of connector C105.

Relay 4 Fuel Pump Relay

Terminal	Description
85	To pin D of connector C101.
86	To ground.
30	Direct to battery voltage.
87	To 1 20A fuse then to the fuel pump

Cooling fans can use two relays or one, depending on the radiator fan setup. Two fans can be on one circuit that run at the same time, or the two fans can be wired to separate circuits, similar to the factory version. One fan functions as a low-speed fan; the other is a high-speed fan, which comes on in the event the engine is not cooling down. Use the low-speed fan relay if running only one fan.

Relay 5 Cooling Fan 1/Slow-Speed Fan	
Terminal	Description
85	To conversion car wiring (a wire that is hot in run and start modes). This wire is typically used to power the original coil. The ballast resistor must be removed.
86	To pin J of connector C100.
30	Direct to battery voltage.
87	To a 20A fuse or larger, depending on the cooling fan requirements.

Relay 6 Cooling Fan 2/High-Speed Fan	
Terminal	Description
85	To conversion car wiring (a wire that is hot in run and start modes). This wire is typically used to power the original coil. The ballast resistor must be removed.
86	To pin H of C100 connector.
30	Direct to battery voltage.
87	To a 20A fuse or larger, depending on the cooling fan requirements.

2009-up LS3 ECM Connector Pinouts

To tune the computer, you need a DLC or an OBDII port. These can be taken from any DLC- or OBDII-equipped car; the salvage yards are full of them. These can be mounted anywhere inside the vehicle. The pins on the port are typically labeled 1 through 16, starting at the top left with 1, and proceeding sequentially with the bottom right pin being 16. The port should be wired as follows:

Pin 2: Serial Data line (purple)
Pin 4: Ground (black)
Pin 5: Ground (black/white)
Pin 9: DLC Serial Data Line
Pin 16: Constant 12 volts (*not* ignition) (orange)

LS3 Factory ECM Pinouts

LS3 ECM Connectors Pinouts

Terminal, Blue, Item C1

Circuit	Pos	Wire Gage	Color	Circuit Description
239M	10	22	Pink	Power
419	12	22	Brown/White	CEL Light
465	13	22	Green/White	Fuse Bus Pos 7A
239	19	18	Pink	Power
1440	20	22	Red/White	Fuse Bus Pos 6G
121	25	22	White	Speed Bulk Head
Pos C				
1164	33	22	White/Black	Pedal Module Pos F
1374	35	22	Red	Pedal Module Pos C
1271	36	22	Brown	Pedal Module Pos D
1272	37	22	Purple	Pedal Module Pos A
818	39	22	Brown	Pin D Bulk Head
5069	40	22	Brown	Fuse Bus Pin 1A
PDL 1	47	22	Blue	Pedal Module Pos E
PDL 2	49	22	Lt. Blue	Pedal Module Pos B
473	54	22	Blue	Fuse Bus 7D
All other positions to have cavity plugs.				

Terminal, Black, Item C2

Circuit	Pos	Wire Gage	Color	Circuit Description
2121	1	22	Purple	Odd Coil Pin G
1664	2	22	Tan	Odd Fr O2 Sensor Pos A
1665	3	22	Purple/White	Odd Fr O2 Sensor Pos B
1876	6	22	Lt. Blue	Even Knock Pos A
407	7	22	Tan	Even Knock Pos B
496	8	22	Blue	Odd Knock Pos A
1716	9	22	Gray	Odd Knock Pos B

581	11	22	Yellow	ETC Pos B
582	12	22	Brown	ETC Pos A
5290	13	18	Pink/Black	Pos 1B Bulk Head
5284	14	22	Purple	Cam Phaser Control Pos D
1746	16	22	Lt. Blue/Black	Injector, 3 Pos B
2128	17	22	Purple/White	Even Coils Pos G
2124	18	22	Green/White	Even Coils Pos C
2130	19	22	Brown/White	Even Coils Pos E
632	23	22	Pink/Black	Cam Sensor Ground Pos B
2755	24	22	Black	Oil Pressure Sensor Rtn Pos A
1868	27	22	Yellow/Black	Crank Sensor Ground Pos B
1704	28	22	Pink/Black	Fuse Cavity 8J
1704A	29	22	Red/White	ETC Pos C
1745	32	22	Lt. Green/Black	Injector 2 Pin B
2127	33	22	Orange	Odd Coil Pos B
2127A	34	22	Green	Odd Coil Pos C
2129	35	22	Brown	Odd Coil Pos E
631	39	22	Orange	Cam Sensor Power Pos A
2705	40	22	Gray	Oil Pressure Sensor 5V Ref

LS3 ECM Connectors Pinouts

Pos B

Circuit	Pos	Wire Gage	Color	Circuit Description
552	42	22	Tan	MAF Pos D
1867	43	22	Lt. Green	Crank Sensor Signal Pos C
1688	44	22	Lt. Blue/Black	ETC Pos E
6753	46	22	Brown	Cam Phaser Low Pin E
878	48	22	Blue/White	Injector 8 Pin B
847	49	22	Tan/White	Injector, 5 Pin B
846	52	22	Yellow/Black	Injector 6 Pin B

2122	53	22	Red/White	Even Coils Pos B
2126	54	22	Lt. Blue/White	Even Coils Pos F
2123	55	22	Lt. Blue	Odd Coils Pin F
633	59	22	Brown/White	Cam Sensor Signal Pos C
331A	60	22	Tan/White	Oil Pressure Sensor Signal
Pos C				
472	62	22	Tan	MAF Pos E
1869	63	22	Blue/White	Crank Sensor Power Pos A
485	64	22	Green	ETC Throttle Pos. Sensor
1 Pos D				
486	66	22	Purple	ETC Throttle Pos. Sensor
2 Pos F				
492	67	22	Yellow	MAF Pos A
3113	68	22	Gray/White	Odd Fr O2 Heater pos E
844	70	22	Lt. Blue/Black	Injector 4 Pin B
877	71	22	Orange/Black	Injector 7 Pin B
1744	72	22	Tan	Injector 1 Pin B
750	73	14	Black	Ground

All other positions to have cavity plugs.

LS3 ECM Connectors Pinouts

Terminal, Gray, Item C3

Circuit	Pos	Wire Gage	Color	Circuit Description
1667	3	22	Tan	Even Fr O2 Pos A
1666	4	22	Purple	Even Fr O2 Pos B
225	7	22	Orange	Generator Pos B
3212	15	22	Lt. Green	Even Fr O2 Pos E
469	23	22	Orange/Black	MAP Pos A
2501	33	22	Tan	ALDL Pin 14
2761	35	22	Tan	ECT Pos 1
2704	39	22	Gray	MAP Pos C
335	49	22	Green	Fuse Bus Pos 7D
2500	53	22	Tan/Black	ALDL Pin 6
410	55	22	Yellow	Engine Coolant Sensor
Pos 2				
432	59	22	Lt. Green	MAP Pos B
321	66	22	Purple/White	VSS TOSS Hi Pos 2
322	67	22	Lt. Green/Black	VSS TOSS Lo Pos 1
750A	73	14	Black Ground	

All other positions to have cavity plugs.

2014-up LT1 ECM Connector Pinouts

Blue Plug J1

Cavity	Circuit	Size (mm)	Color	Circuit Description
	7446	0.5	Lt. Blue/White	Fuel Line Pressure Sensor Signal
	3200	0.5	Yellow/White	Throttle Inlet Absolute Pressure Sensor Signal
5	3201	0.5	White/Red	Throttle Inlet Absolute Pressure Sensor 5V Reference
8	7447	0.5	Black/Yellow	Fuel Line Pressure Sensor, Low Reference
14	1164	0.5	White/Red	Accelerator Pedal Position, 5V Reference (1)
15	1161	0.5	Yellow/White	Accelerator Pedal Position Signal (1)
24	7445	0.5	Brown/Red	Fuel Line Pressure Sensor, 5V Reference
30	1271	0.5	Black/Lt. Blue	Accelerator Pedal Position, Low Reference (1)
33	1274	0.5	Brown/Red	Accelerator Pedal Position, 5V Reference (2)
34	1162	0.5	Lt. Green/White	Accelerator Pedal Position Signal (2)
36	7493A	0.5	Lt. Blue/Black	High Speed GMLAN Serial Data (+)(3)
37	7494A	0.5	White	High Speed GMLAN Serial Data (-)(3)
39	2500	0.5	Lt. Blue	High Speed GMLAN Serial Data (+)(1)
40	2501	0.5	White	High Speed GMLAN Serial Data (-)(1)
42 C	FN2C	0.5	Black/Red	Fan 2 Control
43 C	818	0.75	Brown	Vehicle Speed Output
44	465	0.5	Lt. Green/Gray	Fuel Pump Primary Relay Control
46	419	0.5	Brown/White	Check Engine Indicator Control
51	439A	0.5	Violet/Lt. Green	Run/Crank Ignition, 1 Voltage
52	740	0.5	Red/Yellow	Battery
53	1272	0.5	Black/Violet	Accelerator Pedal Position, Low Reference (2)
59	2366	0.5	White/Black	Cooling Fan Control Relay Speed Signal
60	5291	0.5	Violet/Lt. Blue	Powertrain Main Relay Fused Supply (2)
64 C	20	0.5	Yellow	Top of Travel Clutch Switch
67	5292	0.75	Violet/Lt. Blue	Powertrain Main Relay Fused Supply (3)
72	5991A	0.5	Yellow	Powertrain Relay Coil Control
73	5290B	2.5	Violet/Lt. Blue	Powertrain Main Relay Fused Supply (1)

Black Plug J2

Cavity	Circuit	Size (mm)	Color	Circuit Description
3	2919	0.5	Black/Lt. Green	Fuel Rail Pressure Sensor, Low Reference
6 C	821	0.5	Purple/White	Vehicle Speed Sensor (+)
7 C	822	0.5	Lt. Green/Black	Vehicle Speed Sensor (-)
10	3110	0.5	Violet/Gray	Heated Oxygen Sensor, High Signal Bank 1 Sensor (1)
11	3210	0.5	Violet/White	Heated Oxygen Sensor High Signal Bank 2 Sensor (1)
15	4008	0.5	Brown/Gray	Humidity Sensor Signal
16	582	0.5	Brown/White	Throttle Actuator Control Close
18	2917	0.5	Brown/Red	Fuel Rail Sensor, 5V Reference
19	2918	0.5	Lt. Blue/White	Fuel Rail Pressure Sensor Signal
26	3111	0.5	White/Black	Heated Oxygen Sensor, Low Signal Bank 1 Sensor (1)

Cavity	Circuit	Size (mm)	Color	Circuit Description
27	3211	0.5	Yellow/White	Heated Oxygen Sensor, Low Signal Bank 2 Sensor (1)
32	581	0.5	Yellow	Throttle Actuator Control Open
34	2701	0.5	Brown/Red	Throttle Position Sensor, 5V Reference
36	496	0.75	Violet/Gray	Knock Sensor Signal (1)
37	1876	0.75	White/Gray	Knock Sensor Signal (2)
41	3113	0.5	Gray/White	Heated Oxygen Sensor, Low Control Bank 1 Sensor (1)
43	432	0.5	Lt. Green/White	Manifold Absolute Pressure Sensor Signal
44	2704	0.5	Gray/Red	Manifold Absolute Pressure Sensor, 5V Reference
47 C	121	0.75	White	Engine Speed Output
49	6289	0.5	White/Lt. Blue	Induction Air Temperature Sensor Signal
51	428	0.5	Lt. Green/Lt. Blue	EVAP Canister Purge Solenoid Control
52	492	0.5	Lt. Green/White	Mass Airflow Sensor Signal
53	25A	0.5	Brown	Charge Indicator Control
54	2752	0.5	Black/Brown	Throttle Position Sensor, Low Reference
55	23A	0.5	Gray	Generator Field Duty Cycle Signal
56	1716	0.75	Black/Yellow	Knock Sensor, Low Reference (1)
57	2303	0.75	Black/Gray	Knock Sensor, Low Reference (2)
59	179	0.5	Lt. Blue	Oil Pump Command Signal
61	3212	0.5	Lt. Green/Yellow	Heated Oxygen Sensor Heater, Low Control Bank 2 Sensor (1)
63	469	0.5	Black/Lt. Green	Manifold Absolute Pressure Sensor, Low Reference
69	2760	0.5	Black/Violet	Intake Air Temperature Sensor, Low Reference
70	3630	0.5	Lt. Blue/White	Throttle Position Sensor (SENT1) Signal
73	451	2.5	Black/White	Signal Ground

Gray Plug J3

Cavity	Circuit	Size (mm)	Color	Circuit Description
1	331	0.5	Yellow/Brown	Oil Pressure Sensor Signal
2	2705	0.5	White/Red	Oil Pressure Sensor, 5V Reference
3	2161	0.5	Brown/Yellow	Fuel Rail Pressure Sensor 2 Signal
8	410	0.5	Lt. Blue	Crankshaft 60X Sensor Voltage
10	6270	0.5	Violet/Lt. Blue	Ignition Control (3)
11	2123	0.5	Lt. Green/Lt. Blue	Ignition Control (4)
12	2124	0.5	Yellow/Lt. Blue	Ignition Control (5)
13	2125	0.5	Lt. Blue/Gray	Ignition Control (6)
14	2126	0.5	Brown/Lt. Blue	Ignition Control, Low Reference Bank 2
15	2130	0.5	Black/Gray	High-Pressure Fuel Pump Actuator, High Control
16	7301	0.75	Yellow	Oil Pressure Sensor Low Reference
17	2755	0.5	Black/Violet	High-Pressure Fuel Pump Actuator, High Control
24	2761	0.5	Yellow	Coolant Temperature Sensor, Low Reference
25	6272	0.5	Black/Violet	Crankshaft 60X Sensor Signal
26	6271	0.5	Lt. Green	Crankshaft 60X Sensor, Low Reference
27	2122	0.5	Lt. Blue/White	Ignition Control (2)
28	2127	0.5	Lt. Green/Gray	Ignition Control (7)
29	2128	0.5	Violet/White	Ignition Control (8)
30	2121	0.5	Lt. Blue/Violet	Ignition Control (1)
31	2129	0.5	Black/Lt. Blue	Ignition Control, Low Reference Bank 1
32	7300	0.75	Violet/Black	High-Pressure Fuel Pump Actuator, Low Control
33	5275	0.5	Yellow/Violet	Camshaft Position Intake Sensor (1)
34	5300	0.5	Gray/Lt. Blue	Camshaft Position Intake Sensor Supply Voltage (1)
39	5284	0.5	Violet/Brown	Camshaft Phaser Intake Solenoid (1)
45	4804	0.5	Gray/Lt. Blue	Direct Fuel Injector (DFI), High-Voltage Control Cylinder (4)
46	4802	0.5	Lt. Blue	Direct Fuel Injector (DFI) High-Voltage Control Cylinder (2)
47	4806	0.5	Violet/Lt. Green	Direct Fuel Injector (DFI), High-Voltage Control Cylinder (6)
48	4808	0.5	Gray	Direct Fuel Injector (DFI), High-Voltage Control Cylinder (8)
49	4803	0.5	Lt. Green	Direct Fuel Injector (DFI), High-Voltage Control Cylinder (3)
50	4807	0.5	Yellow/Gray	Direct Fuel Injector (DFI), High-Voltage Control Cylinder (7)
51	4805	0.5	White/Lt. Green	Direct Fuel Injector (DFI), High-Voltage Control Cylinder (5)
52	4801	0.5	Brown	Direct Fuel Injector (DFI), High-Voltage Control Cylinder (1)
53	5301	0.5	Black/Lt. Green	Camshaft Position Intake Sensor, Low Reference
59	6753	0.5	Black/Brown	Camshaft Phaser W Return, Low Reference
65	4904	0.5	Lt. Blue/White	Direct Fuel Injector (DFI), High-Voltage Supply Cylinder (4)
66	4902	0.5	Lt. Blue/Gray	Direct Fuel Injector (DFI), High-Voltage Control Cylinder (2)
67	4906	0.5	Violet/Gray	Direct Fuel Injector (DFI), High-Voltage Control Cylinder (6)
68	4908	0.5	Gray/White	Direct Fuel Injector (DFI), High-Voltage Control Cylinder (8)
69	4903	0.5	Lt. Green/Gray	Direct Fuel Injector (DFI), High-Voltage Control Cylinder (3)
70	4907	0.5	White/Yellow	Direct Fuel Injector (DFI), High-Voltage Control Cylinder (7)
71	4905	0.5	Lt. Green/White	Direct Fuel Injector (DFI), High-Voltage Control Cylinder (5)
72	4901	0.5	Brown/White	Direct Fuel Injector (DFI), High-Voltage Control Cylinder (1)
73	451A	2.5	Black/White	Signal Ground

Aftermarket Harnesses

The following explains the capabilities of a factory LS wiring harness.

Most aftermarket harnesses are purely plug-and-play for simplicity and ease of installation. Therefore, you just plug it in, make four wiring connections, and the engine should fire up. You must know the specifics of your engine and transmission before ordering, however, as there are a lot of options. An unloomed harness allows you to reroute any wires to components that you may have moved.

The data link connector (DLC) or on-board diagnostics (OBDII) port is a must-have for any LS swap, and it is often overlooked when retrofitting a stock harness. Make sure you grab the wiring harness from the donor car. If you don't, you'll have to head back to the salvage yard or take your chances on eBay.

From left to right: K&N air filter, three-pin MAF, 90-degree elbow with three-pin MAF, five-pin MAF. You must match the MAF to your harness.

The pinouts for the later models are included here, but each computer and engine has different requirements for operation. DBW and DOD

You can also use a new factory harness such as this LT1 kit from Chevrolet Performance. It has everything you need and comes from the GM factory supplier.

For the 1969 Chevelle, this kit includes all the connections required and has this fuse box that mounts under the hood. Bolt it down in a convenient location, such as the inner fender well or behind the headlights on the core support.

engines make this more complicated. A pre-made retrofit wiring harness is generally the best solution for any Gen III/IV swap. This puts all the

This black sensor at the rear passenger's side of the block is the reluctor sensor. Black means that this is a 24x engine. If this were gray, it would be 58x.

The alternator has a single trigger wire and it needs to be soldered to the new harness.

The fuel injectors plug into your harness and must match the injector type for your engine. If you find that yours do not match, you need to install adapters or change to the correct connectors for your harness. This is a common issue for performance engines using aftermarket injectors.

This mid-1990s MAF from an LT1 Camaro works with the three-pin LS1 harness that I am installing. It costs $10 at the salvage yard rather than $90 at the parts store, so it's a good value as long as it is in good condition.

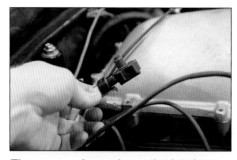

The sensor depends on the intake. Most stock LS intakes use the type shown here. The MAP sensor could be like this GM LS sensor that installs into a port in the intake or you could use a remote-mount MAP sensor.

The idle air control (IAC) valve modulates the incoming air at idle to keep the engine running smooth in idle conditions. The stock IAC installed into the Holley 90-mm throttle body and the harness plugged in directly.

For DBC engines, the throttle position sensor (TPS) plugs into the side of the throttle body.

When it comes to hardwiring, several loose wires must be properly connected. This ignition wire needs 12 volts in the run and start position to power the ECM during startup.

These wires are optional, but in regard to safety, they should be connected. The neutral safety switch connects to the safety switch on the shifter, either auto or manual. If you don't have one, you probably should install one. The other wire runs to the brake light switch.

These wires are for the oil pressure, tach, and check engine light. LS ECMs put out a 4-cylinder signal to the tach, which must be modulated for stock tachs. Sometimes you must use a pull-up resistor (10,000 ohm), which bridges between the tach feed wire and a 12-volt source, providing adequate voltage for the tach to trigger.

I used the factory wire loom to route the wires across the firewall and down to the battery.

Modern drivetrains are electronic, so proper grounds to the transmission are vital. A simple braided ground strap to the frame will do, and it also helps reduce electrolysis in the cooling system.

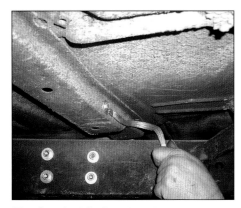

For the electrical system to correctly operate, the body needs to be grounded. Scrape the paint away from the metal at the grounding point for solid contact and proper ground.

responsibility in the hands of technicians who have tested each harness and guarantee it is correct.

If the harness is incorrectly wired in any way, it can overload and ruin the stock computer, rendering it useless. In addition, purchasing an aftermarket wiring harness affords the luxury of troubleshooting tech assistance. If you have trouble with an aftermarket harness, a quick

call to the tech line might save you some valuable time and money, and potentially a dead computer. The plug-and-play nature of an aftermarket harness combined with the relative affordability makes it the best option, plus they generally look better than a hacked-up stock harness. Another thing to consider is that many factory harnesses are older, and with age wiring becomes brittle and corroded. An aftermarket harness is all new, so the swap gets more life out of the wires. It's also impossible to know if the computer and harness were removed with care or yanked out, which can damage the wires and connectors.

Many aftermarket sources offer harnesses, and there are far too many to include in this book. Painless Performance offers a great harness that simplifies the process of wiring the LS-series engine. Chevrolet Performance offers harnesses that go along with their ECMs for swaps as well.

Most aftermarket harnesses have similar connections; the finer points of finish and overall look are what separate them. Many aftermarket harnesses are left in loose form; that is, without any loom or wrap on the wires. Certain wires are grouped together for their placement on the

engine, such as the fuel injector harnesses, but that is as far as it goes. This leaves it up to you to cover the harness for the final finish. Other brands of aftermarket harnesses group each set of wires together as they would be on an engine and complete the job with wire loom or tape, making it a clean, out-of-the-box installation. If any stock components have been changed or moved to another location, the harness may have to be altered, so that is something to think about before ordering.

To select the correct aftermarket harness, you need to determine engine model, power control module (PCM), transmission model, MAF sensor, drive-by-cable (DBC) or DBW system, and the type of fuel injector to be used. First, identify the engine and computer, whether it's an automatic or a manual transmission and if the transmission is electronically controlled. Older automatics such as the TH350 and manuals, including the Muncie M22, are not electronically controlled. However, newer-generation automatic transmissions such as the 4L60E automatic are electronically controlled. It's important to recognize this because the transmission must be connected to the ECU or PCM.

For the Buick GS, mounting the underhood fuse box was an issue. It fits in very few places. I chose to locate the box on the passenger-side fender, next to the battery.

I drilled three holes in the fender to match three holes that I drilled into the back of the box. The box does not have any mounting tabs or a bracket; you are on your own.

I bolted the box to the fender using large fender washers for support. Although the box looks crooked, it is parallel with the ground, as the top of the fender is angled downward.

The fuse center pops into the box frame, along with all the wires. This location allows you to run most of the wires behind the fender for a clean install.

With the cover on, the fusebox looks as if it belongs there. For the A-Body, this location is about the only place it fits and looks good. The wiring harness is just long enough to fit here as well.

There is not much room in this corner, just enough for the ECM, battery, and fuse center. Only one wire loom has to run along the inner fender.

I made an 8-gauge wire to connect the fuse box to the battery. This wire attaches to a large lug on the bottom of the box. The two lugs on the front are for accessories.

The 8-gauge wire connects directly to the Optima battery on the positive (+) post.

The main harness loom is not long enough to go behind the fender, so I secured it to the inner fender with some wire clamps, just like the factory loom. I ran the ECM connectors behind the fender.

The MAF sensor is either a 3- or 5-pin (make sure to get this from the donor vehicle). Determining if the throttle body is DBC or DBW is essential as well.

The type of fuel injector is the last piece of component information needed. Three main types are available: Bosch EV1 (the older LS style uses a metal bale clip, commonly referred to as a "minitimer"), Bosch EV6, and Delphi USCAR Flex Fuel injector. LS engines are plug-and-play for just about every connector, so installing the harness is quite simple.

Once the engine is wired up, those pesky little accessories such as gauges

These wiring components must go inside the car: the DLC port, ignition wire, pedal wires, and accessory harness.

I used a large factory hole in the firewall to route these wires. Make sure you use a grommet, as bare metal and wires do not mix.

still need to be connected. Because the vehicles in which these engines were originally installed were so heavily dependent on the computer system, all the gauges were routed through the computer. Although you could swap in the gauges from a donor car, swapping requires significant modification to retrofit late-model computer controlled gauges. A cable-driven speedometer does not do much good with a vehicle speed sensor (VSS) wire attached to it; neither does the factory tach with the LS tach wire plugged into it. Special considerations must be made to get information from the engine to the driver.

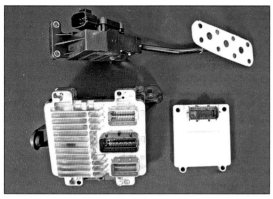

Each DBW engine requires its own specific pedal, throttle body, and possibly a TAC module. This is a Vortec pedal and TAC module for a 2003 1500. The small box to the lower right is the transmission control module (TCM).

The LT1, Gen IV, and some Gen III LS engines use DBW throttle control. The LT1 has an all-in-one pedal while the others use a separate TAC module. To mount the pedal under the dash, I modified the factory pedal bracket with some 1 x 1–inch square tubing for spacers.

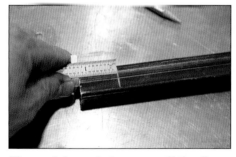

The pedal needs to come off the firewall about 1.25 inches at the bottom, so I marked that length on the tubing and cut it.

To get the angle right, I marked the rise on the bench and measured it. A 4-degree drop from bottom to top seemed to fit the firewall best. You could just cut the spacers flat, but that is not as clean.

I removed the bracket from the pedal and bolted each spacer in place.

I welded each spacer to the bracket. I also welded the large flat washers in place to keep the holes lined up. Then I painted the bracket.

I marked and cut the three spacers for orientation and placement. The spacers ensure enough travel for the pedal to reach WOT.

I used the upper left hole for the factory pedal mount and the lower bolt hole for the new pedal. Once the pedal was vertical, I drilled the other holes in the firewall and bolted it in place.

The LT1 harness pedal plug locks into the pedal and that is all there is to it. Nice and simple.

These coil packs for a Gen III/IV engine are in good condition. The failure rate is small on these coils, so replacing them isn't necessary. The left example is for a 1999–2004 car and 1998–2003 truck. The one on the right is for a 1999–2006 4.8, 5.3, and 6.0 truck and 2003–2006 Hummer. Not shown are 2005-up car and truck coils. The terminals are different on all of them.

The coil packs for Gen III/IV engines are very good and have a very low failure rate, so there is no need to replace them in most cases. On the left is a coil pack for a 1999–2004 car or 1998–2003 truck; on the right is a coil pack for a 1999–2006 4.8, 5.3, 6.0 truck, or 2003–2006 hummer. Not shown are 2005–up car and truck coils. The terminals are different on all three. If you do not have coils, you need to source them. You could go with stock coils or aftermarket. I have an LS1 harness for the Chevelle, but it does not match the Vortec truck coils. This can be a costly mistake because coils are not cheap.

These MSD LS1 coils match the harness. Make sure you order the right ones for your harness and mounts. Aftermarket coils are commonly available for all three coil versions, but you have to verify which ones you need.

The coil pack mounts are another potential problem, so you need to pay attention. The mount frames and valvecovers are different for each coil design. Make sure your coils match your frames, valvecovers, and wiring harness. This is why securing every component from the donor vehicle is important and building your own engine without a donor becomes costly.

Tachometers are simple gauges that measure the revolutions per minute of the engine. Although not absolutely necessary they are useful, especially in manual transmission cars. If you drive a car aggressively, you need to know how hard the engine is being worked. Getting the tach signal to an old stock tach requires an adapter. The signal is modulated at a different rate than that of a typical V-8 tach. The LS signal must be converted to a standard signal with a module. These modules are available from Dakota Digital.

The Dakota Digital SGI-8 module converts the tach signal to different settings, such as 4- or 6-cylinder. The tach signal coming from the LS1 is representative of a 4-cylinder signal. Therefore, a factory 6- or 8-cylinder tach must use this module to read the correct signal and display the proper reading. Programmable tachometers such as an Autometer or VDO unit, do not need this module because they can be set to read a 4-cylinder tach signal.

The speedometer is a similar story. With an electronically controlled transmission, an electronic speedometer can receive the signal from the VSS system via the computer; an aftermarket speedometer can receive a direct signal from the VSS system. If the stock cable-driven speedometer is being used with a late-model transmission, the transmission

Clearance for the coil packs to the A/C box can be an issue. There is very little room between the box and the rear coil on the passenger's side. Factory coils are a touch smaller than these MSDs, but some factory units have a very long plug terminal. It clears, but it is tight. Remote-mount coil packs solve this issue.

I applied silicone paste on the ceramic wire boots used on these Accel spark plug wires. This makes removing the wires from the plugs much easier. The ceramic boots don't melt if they touch the headers.

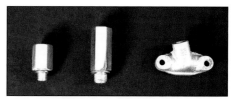

These sensor adapters are required for engine monitoring that is not wired to the ECM. From left to right are coolant temperature, oil pressure at the block, and oil bypass adapter.

These new MSD coils and Accel wires looks great on the 5.3, nice and tidy with added spark voltage.

must be adapted to drive the cable. For 4L60E and T56 OEM transmissions, this is not a huge problem. You can find cable drive tailshafts to replace the original tailshaft. Most aftermarket transmissions already have a cable-drive provision.

The oil-sending unit also requires adapting. The oil cooler bypass fitting on the oil pan just above the oil filter is an ideal place to install an oil pressure fitting for the sending unit. Depending on the specific engine,

select one of three bypass fitting options: a drilled and tapped fitting, a blank boss fitting that can be drilled and tapped, and a dome-top fitting.

The 1997–2004 Corvette engines have a drilled and tapped 1/4-inch pipe thread from the factory, and the 1998–2002 F-Body pans have a boss, but it is not drilled or tapped. The 2005-and-up engines have a domed cap with no boss. Any of these can be used.

If you need to drill and tap the fitting, simply drill it and tap it to the

thread size required by the oil sender fitting. You can also use the 16-mm threaded hole behind the intake manifold with an adapter that converts to 1/8-, 1/4-, 3/8-, or 1/2-inch NPT threads for the oil pressure sending unit.

Performance Project: Drive-by-Wire to Drive-by-Cable Conversion

Information and photos courtesy of Brenden Patten

The drive-by-wire (DBW) system is potentially the most confusing portion of the wiring conversion. Although all engines require a specific pedal and throttle body, some setups require a throttle actuator control (TAC) module and others do not. Each engine using the DBW system requires a pedal, and in some cases a TAC module. In most cases, DBW components are not interchangeable. The pedal, TAC module, and throttle body must remain with the engine for it to work properly. Vortec truck modules are the only interchangeable components, but the ECM needs to be reflashed with a new program as well.

Component packages vary by vehicle. The 1997–2004 Cor-

vette uses a pedal and separate TAC module to operate the specific throttle body. In 2005, General Motors went to a DBW pedal that incorporated the TAC sensor in the pedal, so only the pedal and throttle body is needed for a swap. The same goes for the 2005–2006 GTO, which uses a specific GTO pedal-only configuration. SSR trucks use a dedicated DBW pedal with a TAC module. The Cadillac CTS-V uses a pedal and TAC module up to 2004, when it switched to a pedal only in 2005-up. The 2007 Trailblazer uses a pedal only and is different from the rest of the trucks.

Vortec-powered trucks with the adjustable pedal system are not suitable and must be adapted for use with conversion engines. These trucks use a DBW pedal mounted on a moving

1 DBW is not the solution for every engine package and application. However, converting a DBW engine to DBC is not exactly easy. Some ECMs can be converted to DBW.

2 You can remove the back of the ECM case to look for this section of the board.

3 If the ECM board does not have pins soldered into this location, it is not a conversion candidate.

Wiring Conversion

Wire Color/Sensor Pin Location	Description ECM Plug/Pin Location	Throttle Position Sensor (factor pin location for 2003–up DBC Express van)
Pin A or 1 - Gray	5-volt reference	Blue pin 8
Pin B or 2 - Black	Low reference	Blue pin 60
Pin C or 3 - Dark Blue	TP Signal	Green pin 24

Oil Pressure Sensor (2003–up harnesses)		
Pin A or 1 - Black	Low reference	Blue pin 63
Pin B or 2 - Gray	5-volt reference	Blue pin 7
Pin C or 3 - Tan/White	Oil pressure signal	Green pin 58

Wire - IAC Pin	Description	PCM Plug/Pin Location
Idle Air Controller Valve		
Light green/black pin A	IAC coil B low	Green pin 77
Light green/white pin B	IAC coil B high	Green pin 76
Light Blue/black pin C	IAC coil A low	Green pin 78
Light Blue/white pin D	IAC coil A high	Green pin 79

platform that adjusts to the height of the driver. Of course, you could simply swap to a cable-driven throttle body or a carbureted setup for one of these engines.

The trucks' pedals and TAC modules are very confusing; General Motors seemed to do a lot of different things with the trucks over the years. DBW was first available in the trucks in 1999, and there have been many different pedals with and without TAC modules. Therefore, it's important to get all the components from the donor vehicle beforehand. If you didn't get the pedal that goes with the engine (not everybody thinks to grab the gas pedal when pulling an engine), you can pur-

chase one from any GM dealer, salvage yard, or even a few aftermarket shops, but you need all the details for your engine and ECM.

Converting a DBW ECM to operate a DBC application is possible, but not all DBW ECMs are capable of making the switch. The following ECMs are known to be DBW/DBC compliant:

- 1999–2002 Serv. No. 09354896, 12200411: All blue/red connector PCMs work with either DBW or DBC with the correct programming installed.
- 2003 Serv. No. 12576106 with Hwd. No. 12570558: Most 2003 trucks use this PCM, but not all.
- 2004 Serv. No. 12586243 with Hwd. No. 12583659: Most GTOs, Express vans, and Cadillac CTS-Vs use this PCM, as well as Caddy CTS-V, and some trucks.
- 2005–2006 Serv. No. 12589462 with Hwd. No. 12589161: Found in Express vans and some trucks.
- 2007 Serv. No. 12602801 with Hwd. No. 12589161: Found only in Express vans.

If your ECM does not have these numbers, you can check it by removing the back cover and looking for the location on the circuit board, labeled B67U1. If that location has pins soldered to the board, then it has the controller needed to be DBC. If not, then it cannot be used.

The issue with going from DBW to DBC is that the DBC requires the controller for the idle air control (IAC) valve. The controller opens and closes the valve when needed. Most truck ECMs do not support DBC conversion. All DBW ECMs require reprogramming to be used for DBC applications.

Wiring the DBW computer requires adding the IAC and throttle position sensor (TPS) wires. The 2003–up oil pressure plug works for the TPS, but the IAC uses its own plug, so that needs to be sourced.

The wire color and location match 2003–up Express vans that had mechanical DBC throttle bodies. You can use the oil pressure sensor plug from a 2003–up harness for the TPS. Pay attention that the 5-volt reference and low reference are opposite between oil pressure and TPS.

If you use the oil pressure plug for TPS, you need to switch the black and gray wires at the TPS plug or switch the black and gray wires at the PCM. If you don't switch them, the TPS works backward.

Finally, move the Oil Pressure Signal wire (tan/white) from the green pin 58 to the green pin 4.

Also, the exact location that the TPS receives its 5-volt reference from does not matter; it could come from pin 7 or 8. The same goes for the low reference; it could come from pin 60 or 63. What *is* important is that the TPS has 5-volt reference and low reference at the correct locations at the sensor.

If converting from DBW to DBC on a red/blue harness, you only need to add the wiring for the IAC valve and TPS.

For 1999–2002, power and ground are fed directly to the oxygen sensor heaters.

If you have a red/blue connector PCM, you can use it on a 2003–up harness (green/blue connector) with a cable throttle, with a few simple modifications. The only other thing that needs alteration is the oxygen sensor wiring. On the 2003–up green/blue connector PCMs, the PCM supplies a ground for the oxygen sensor heaters, and 12v-plus comes from the fuse block.

To modify a 2003–up green/blue harness to work with a blue/red computer follow the steps below:

Remove the blue PCM connector pins 24, 27, 64, and 67. These should be black with white stripes. These were extra ground wires provided to the 2003–up PCM so it could control ground to the oxygen heaters. The 1999–2002 PCM does not

Oxygen Sensor Pinouts

Bank 1 Sensor 1 - black/white - green connector pin 72
Bank 1 Sensor 2 - brown - green connector pin 52 - after CAT oxygen sensor
Bank 2 Sensor 1 - light green - green connector pin 74
Bank 2 Sensor 2 - red/white - green connector pin 53 - after CAT oxygen sensor

need these. Just pull the pins out. Don't cut anything yet; you need to hook these to a few other wires pulled out of the PCM connectors.

Next remove the wires from the PCM connector that go to the oxygen sensor heater control. There are four wires, one for each oxygen sensor. If you are using only front oxygen sensors in your conversion, omit anything to do with Sensor 2.

Now you should have four ground wires, and two (or four) oxygen sensor heater control wires pulled from the PCM connectors.

Locate the four tan oxygen sensor low-reference wires going into the blue PCM connector. If using only front oxygen sensors, it's blue pins 26 and 29. If also using rear oxygen sensors, add pins 25 and 28.

These wires are always tan and may have a white stripe. The easiest way to splice these together is to pull the pin out (note its location), remove some insulation with a stripper, solder on the new wire, and then tape up the solder joint. You might be able to use heat shrink tubing as well.

Then reinstall the pin in its original location. Leave about 12 inches of wire loose for each wire you splice into. Do this for all oxygen sensors.

You should have four loose black/white ground wires. You have two to four oxygen sensor heater control wires and two to four wires going to each of the tan wires. All these wires must be hooked together in a big splice pack.

Using a piece of 1/4- or 5/16-inch shrink tubing, slide the tubing over all four ground wires, several inches past the ends to be soldered. Next, strip off about an inch of insulation from the wires. Start hooking them together end to end; you should be able to solder them together and slip the heat shrink over them when done.

The last step is making the connectors fit inside the PCM. To do this, cut the rib off the green plastic terminal cover so it fits in the red PCM socket. You need to use oxygen sensors for a 2002 Chevy truck (5.3L); it is a white plastic connector that plugs right into the 2003-and-newer harness without changing plugs.

ENGINE MANAGEMENT SYSTEMS, TUNING SOFTWARE AND CONTROLLERS

Each engine requires its own computer, and the programming must match the engine, so you can't just swap computers even if the plugs are the same type. General Motors produces several computer types and each is built for a specific engine group. Some work with many engines, and some only work with one. It is very important to obtain the original computer, harness, and sensors when buying a used engine. This ensures that you have everything needed to make the swap as simple as possible.

Of course, if you are buying a crate engine or can't get all the

Carbureted LS engines are distributorless, so you need an ignition controller, such as this one from FAST. The XIM is also used with the XFI system on EFI engines. (Photo Courtesy FAST)

original components, the aftermarket provides the necessary parts. The aftermarket offers engine management systems for both EFI and carbureted engines (carbureted LS engines available from Chevrolet Performance as crate engines or carb-converted Gen III/IV engines). The possibilities are almost endless.

The 24- and 58-tooth are the two main type of reluctor wheels. The reluctor wheel is mounted to the crankshaft at the rear and inside of the block. The crank position (CKP) sensor is mounted behind the start and to the right rear of the block. As

the crankshaft rotates, the teeth on the reluctor wheel interrupt the magnetic field that the sensor has created. This sensor records these interruptions and sends a signal to the computer; these signals are used to detect misfires, detonation, or other problems with the ignition system.

You need to identify whether you have a 24x or 58x reluctor. A quick check for this is to look at the reluctor wheel sensor. A black sensor means you have a 24x wheel and a gray sensor means you have a 58x wheel. The 2014–up Gen V LT-series engines all have a black 58x sensor.

The 24-tooth reluctor wheel is found on the 1997–2004 Corvette LS1 or LS6 (all were DBW), 2005 LS2 Corvette, 1998–2002 Camaro/Firebird, 2004 LS1 GTO, 2005–2006 LS2 GTO, 2004–2006 SSR (LS2 and 5.3 liter), and 1999–2006 4.8-, 5.3-, and 6.0-liter Vortec truck engines.

The 58-tooth reluctor wheel is found on DBW engines only, so it cannot be used with DBC without modifications. If you want to run these engines with a traditional throttle cable, they need to be converted to a 24-tooth reluctor wheel,

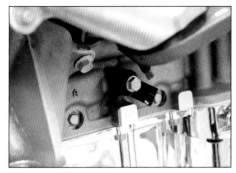

The ECM must operate the reluctor wheel that it originally came with; it can't be changed to operate a different reluctor wheel. You can change the reluctor wheel setup, but you must have the corresponding computer. Gray sensors are 58x, and black sensors are 24x.

The 1997–1998 LS1 Y- and F-Body computer is different from the later LS1 ECM. The pinouts and the wiring harnesses are different. This is a 1998 Camaro ECM, front and back side.

Later ECMs for 1999–2002 LS1s look different, and they are. The wires are in different places. Do not try to wire an early harness to a later ECM; it won't work.

Until recently, the 2004–2005 ECMs were capable of only DBW, but several programmers have figured out how to reprogram that portion of the ECM. This allows you to install a less complicated DBC throttle body on a 2004–2005 LS engine.

This 58x-reluctor computer and the ancillary parts are very expensive. Make sure you have them all from the donor car; otherwise you will spend a lot of money to buy these components individually.

The LT-series ECM works for all V-8 versions of the 2014–2016 Gen V engine. You also need a special mount because there are no provisions for mounting the ECM.

along with a 2005 cam gear on the front of the engine, and a 24-tooth reluctor wheel computer.

The alternative to an expensive conversion is to use a converter module such as the TRG-002 from Lingenfelter Performance. This electronic box converts the 58x crank signal and 4x camshaft signal into the 24x and 1x signals used by the 24x ECM, allowing the installer to use DBC and to mix and match ECMs and engines.

The following engines have the 58-tooth reluctor: 2006–up Corvette LS7, 2008–up Corvette LS3, 2007–up 4.8, 5.3, and 6.0 Vortec truck engines.

Changing the reluctor wheel also requires changing the cam timing gear. These two work together to monitor the ignition system. If they don't match or communicate with each other, the engine won't run.

GM Engine ECU Part Number

The following is a list of service part numbers for ECU computers.

Year	Make and Model	Part Number
1997–1998	Corvette, Camaro, Firebird, and Vortec engines	16238212, 16232148 (red and blue plugs)
1999–2000	Corvette, Camaro, Firebird, and Vortec engines	09354896, 16263494
2001–2002	Camaro, Firebird, Vortec, 2001–2003 Corvette LS1 and LS6	12200411
2003	Vortec truck engines	12576106
2004	Corvette LS1 and LS6	12586242
2004	Vortec truck engines	12586243
2004	GTO and SSR	12598343
2005	GTO and SSR	12603892
2005	Corvette LS2	12597191, 12597883.
2005–2006	Vortec truck engines	125862432
2006	Vortec truck engines	12583560, 12583561
2006	5.3 SSR	12596679
2006–2007	LS2 and LS7	12603892
2007–up	Vortec truck engines	12597121

Each engine within the two groups uses a specific computer. The wiring harnesses are dedicated to each computer, so it's very important to get all components when pulling an engine from a salvage vehicle.

The 24x ECMs can be programmed for either DBC or DBW. For instance, a 1999 F-Body LS1 with a DBC throttle body can be wired to a 2000 Corvette DBW ECM, but the ECM must be reprogrammed to reflect the DBC change.

And there's a second option. You can convert an engine to DBC by reprogramming the original computer for DBW, as long as that ECM is DBW compatible (see Chapter 6). You must be able to plug the wiring harness into the computer. The 1998 F-Body computers and harnesses are not compatible with 1999 and later harnesses or computers because the plugs are different. If you plan to run the stock harness and computer, either get them from the donor vehicle or buy used.

Several methods are available for programming the stock ECM. Home-based programs such as HP Tuners and EFI Live are available and designed to work with the Gen III/IV computers. Most aftermarket tuning modules and software are locked, meaning they lock themselves to a particular computer on the first use. To unlock them, you must purchase pass codes or VINs for additional vehicles. Some products include two pass codes to tune two separate vehicles. Typically, when you purchase tuning software, you have unlimited tuning capability or tunes on the same vehicle.

Aftermarket Tuning Packages

Many DIY or home-based tuning packages are intuitive, easy to use, and very efficient. They allow you to tune the engine for a multitude of parameters, help identify trouble codes, and add personalization to the engine. But home-based tuning software can't do everything. Most software packages can't make significant changes to the programming of an ECM, so you can tune the engine, but you cannot change the ECM from DBW to DBC or vice versa. The software also is not the best way to swap a computer from a different year to a different engine; this requires more significant programming beyond what the tuning software was designed for. These programs are great for what they do: tune the existing programming to better suit your application and needs.

HP Tuners

This comprehensive tuning software allows you to tune and adjust every aspect of the stock ECM. Available in base or pro forms, the HP VCM Suite adjusts Gen III/IV computers. This package works on the credit system: choose to tune up to four vehicles, unlimited tunes for the same year and model vehicle (any 2000 Camaro LS1, for example), or unlimited Gen III/IV vehicles. Whichever option you choose costs credits. A single vehicle license costs 2 credits, a year and a model license costs 6 credits, and unlimited LS1 tunes cost 70 credits. The basic software purchase includes 8 credits, and additional credits are always available, adding to the flexibility of the software. This home-based software costs a good deal more than a handheld tuner or shipping your computer, but it has much more flexibility and will likely be worth the extra cost in the end.

However, the HP tuner software cannot load programming from different model years to a given computer. Therefore, you need to start with the right year computer for your engine application. Considered by many to be the most comprehensive tuning software publicly available, HP Tuners software is an excellent choice. The HP Tuner Suite comes with the handheld scanner required to upload the tunes to the vehicle, but the handheld does not come preloaded with tunes. The software gives you access to hundreds of tunes, and you can build your own. The product you buy today will not be the same as it will be in two months, but HP Tuner software is easy to upgrade for up-to-date information and calibrations.

EFI Live

EFI Live offers several versions of its FlashScan products including FlashScan and Tune. The tuning version allows you to build your own ECM tunes, controlling all aspects of the ECM programming. The FlashScan software works on a VIN licensing system, which requires each vehicle to be licensed. The main kit includes two VIN licenses and additional licenses can be purchased.

The EFI Live software is capable of tuning both Gen III and Gen IV computers. The FlashScan software features more than 600 engine calibrations for in-depth ECM tuning, as well as fixes for issues with stock

computers such as vehicle anti-theft system (VATS), MAF, and transmission control system (TCS) fault codes. The software is constantly upgrading and evolving, ensuring the product you purchase remains up-to-date as technology changes.

Handheld Tuners

These are an alternative to home-based software programs and offer more portability for tuning the engine. Handheld engine tuners allow you to tune the computer on the fly and run diagnostics whenever the need strikes, regardless of location. Upper-end handheld tuners are comparable in price to entry-level home-based software programmers. Handhelds usually control the basic functions and parameters of an engine tune, but only the basics; computer-based software programs have many more variables and options. The biggest advantage of handheld tuners is their ease of use. The simple user interface makes tuning easier than with home-based software.

If you need to change from DBW to a throttle cable or swap a newer ECM to an older engine, you need to work with a reprogrammer. Shops such as Speartech offer reprogramming services, so you can precisely program the ECM to your require-

ments. If you plan to keep a stock or slightly modified tune in the computer, sending the stock ECM to be reconfigured is usually cheaper than buying a tuning package. It is also the only way to make certain changes. Some wiring harness dealers such as Painless Performance offer complimentary basic ECM tuning with the purchase of a harness.

When completing a project with a "take-out" engine, other considerations need to be addressed. Most vehicles built with Gen III/IV engines use the ECM to control automatic transmissions, but not all. The LS2 GTO uses a transmission control module (TCM) to send information to the PCM. You must have both components if you are going to use the stock computer. The Vortec platforms began using the TCM on all automatic transmission trucks in 2005. If you change the style of transmission, auto to manual or vice

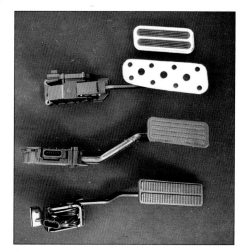

Several DBW pedals are available for LS engines. Shown from left to right are a 2005–up Corvette, 2005–2006 SSR, 2005–2006 GTO, and Lokar pedal replacement pad. Not shown are the 1997–2004 Corvette pedal, the CTS-V, the 2007 Trailblazer, and the rest of the trucks, which interchanged throughout the years.

Tuning your aftermarket ECM is easy with supplied software. Some have simple programs using pre-programmed maps and some are full-blown custom tuning packages that allow the tuner to control every aspect of the tune. For factory computers, HP Tuners software is the most complete aftermarket software available to consumers because it allows you to change just about all parameters of the ECM programming. (Photo Courtesy HP Tuners)

Mounting a stock ECM can be tricky because they do not have mounting holes from the factory. You can use one of the factory assembly brackets or make a bracket. I made this bracket from 14-gauge aluminum and bolted it to the cooling fins. This is a 2003 truck computer.

I bolted each bracket to the ECM case with 1/4-inch bolts.

The upper mount is a little more complicated and I made it from 14-gauge aluminum. This piece is equal length to the Dirty Dingo ECM clamshell. The ECM mount tab is 1¼ inches tall, and the core-support side is 2 inches tall and located at a factory hole in the core support beside the inner headlamp.

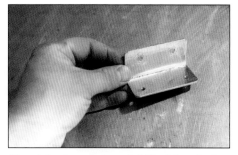

I bent the bracket and drilled four holes. The bracket needs to be big enough to support the ECM and no larger. This one is approximately 3 inches long with each tab about 1½ inches tall.

With the tabs secured to the ECM, I bolted the computer to the steel inner fender of the 1969 Chevelle.

I bolted together the brackets and ECM base and painted them semi-gloss black to match the core support.

versa, the tune should be changed in the computer. If you run an electronically controlled automatic, such as a 4L60E, use the tuning software to enter the VIN number (on the side of the case) into the ECM or TCM

The tricky part is modifying the computer case for bolt-on mounting tabs. I drilled small 1/8-inch pilot holes and then stepped up to 1/4 inch for the bolts.

The heat sinks for the LT1 and some other LS-series ECMs are not large enough for the previous type of mounting. If this is the case, you need a clamshell mount such as the one offered by Dirty Dingo. It works great for flat surfaces, but I need to mount the ECM in open space on the Buick GS. I bent the lower bracket at a 45-degree angle to match the core support on the GS. It is 16-gauge steel.

so the computer has access to the transmission.

The 2014–up Gen V LT-series ECMs do not have transmission controls built in. If you use an electronically controlled transmission, you need a separate transmission controller. Chevrolet Performance offers its Connect & Cruise TC-2 TCU system for 4LXX-series transmissions. There is a kit for 4L6X/7X units, and one for 4L8X transmissions. The TCU plugs into the ECM so that the two controllers can talk to each other. These transmission controllers also work with

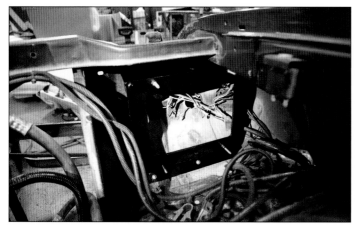

I installed the base in the core support on the passenger's side. I screwed the lower mounts into the sheet metal; the upper mount is a 1/4-inch bolt.

I installed the ECM into the clamshell and bolted it down. I left the top ring raw aluminum.

E-Rod and other Chevrolet LS ECMs.

If you do not run the stock computer and use an electronic transmission, the engine management system may not support the transmission. In this situation you need a transmission controller. Several aftermarket transmission controllers are available, such as the TCI TCU and Painless Performance's Perfect Torc, which gives you greater tuning capability for the GM electronically controlled transmission than does the factory controller. These units are compatible with most GM electronically controlled automatic transmissions. They provide load, gear, RPM, and speed-based programming with the click of a mouse.

The TCI unit is fully compatible with CAN 2.0B engine management systems, such as the FAST XFI system, which makes it easy to integrate the TCU with the engine controller.

Transmission controllers come with tuning software and wiring harnesses. The software allows you to change many parameters, even allowing paddle and push-button shifting configurations and manifold-pressure-based shift firmness, greatly enhancing transmission tuning capa-

bilities far beyond those of the stock TCM or ECM.

Aftermarket Engine Management

The capabilities of aftermarket engine management far exceed those of factory computers. Some builders say that the stock computer is more than enough to control their LS engine, and that's the case for a mostly stock engine. Aftermarket engine management opens an array of tuning options. The factory computer works well for a stock engine, and simple, beneficial tuning changes and adjustments are made easily. However, the stock computer simply can't keep up to a modified

engine fitted with a big cam, supercharger, or turbo.

Mild performance mods such as exhaust, a larger throttle body, and mild cams can be tuned in with the stock computer, but once you get out of the mild performance arena and into more serious mods, or a bunch of smaller components that add up to bigger gains, the stock computer starts to show weakness. The computer can't adjust the fuel maps and timing curves to compensate for new air and fuel requirements on heavily modified engines.

Aftermarket controllers are an important consideration when using a crate engine. The Chevrolet Performance crate engines do not come with a computer or wire harness,

The TCI EZ-TCU transmission controller allows you to manage shift timing, speedometer output, pressures, and a whole host of other options. The unit comes with a dash-mountable controller for quick changes without a laptop. The system is even set up to handle paddle-shifters. (Photo Courtesy TCI)

leaving it up to the buyer to acquire them. However, Chevrolet Performance offers a very good controller and harness for each of its crate engines, including one for the carbureted LS364 and LS376 engines.

Chevrolet Performance Plug-and-Play Engine Controller

General Motors designed these controllers to help take the guesswork out of a Gen III/IV engine swap. Offered for the Gen IV series engines, the controllers work with the LS2 (PN 19166568), LS3 (PN 19201861), and LS7 (PN 19166567) crate engines. They are complete standalone systems that allow the builder to simply plug the factory-style wire harness connections into the new controller and start the engine; no tuning, no removing codes or parameters. Just fire it up. It's a great option for builders who want a factory-based system and a specialized tune for a crate engine.

The Chevrolet Performance controller is based on the factory ECM but features custom calibration of the electronic throttle control, EFI, and ignition systems. The Gen IV controller features an OEM-style fuse and relay center with additional positions for other electronic components, and a 12-wire bulkhead with outputs for the tachometer, VSS, oil pressure, Malfunction Indicator Light (MIL), water temperature, and several others. These signal outputs are compatible with aftermarket gauges only and do not control factory electronic gauges. The cooling fans and fuel pump can be controlled through the controller as well with the included outputs.

Each controller comes with a compatible DBW gas pedal and MAF and oxygen sensors. This controller regulates any LS-series engine that uses the Gen IV air/fuel components. The Chevrolet Performance controller gives you the benefit of the vast testing labs available to General Motors, ensuring flawless performance with aftermarket components. It is also backed by the Chevrolet Performance warranty.

Chevrolet Performance LSX Ignition Controller

Although all OEM-installed engines are fuel injected, not all LS engines are fuel injected. Chevrolet Performance offers two carbureted LS engines for those who like the simplicity of a carburetor. The LS364/440 and LS376/515 engines are based on the LS2 and LS3, respectively, but are cammed up and topped off with Chevrolet Performance's carburetor LS intake. The LS376/515 is the most powerful LS crate engine to date, pushing 515 hp at the flywheel.

Although these powerhouse engines run a classic carb on top, they use the LS distributorless ignition, which means that they need an ignition controller. The Chevrolet Performance LSX ignition controller module (PN 19171130) was developed for use with these carbureted engines and works for any carbureted LS engine with a 58x reluctor wheel. The controller has several pre-programmed timing curves along with software to create custom curves and adjust the rev limiters and step retard functions. The controller includes the MAP sensor and is compatible with all LS-series ignition coils.

If you want to increase the tuning potential of your LS engine, there are quite a few options. The current entry-level controller for LS-series engines features self-learning tuning, which greatly simplifies any LS swap. Self-learn ECMs use data collected by the sensors to constantly tweak how the engine runs, eliminating the finer points of EFI engine tuning.

If you buy a used engine, the wiring harness, computers, and other equipment are often included, giving you all the necessary engine controls. If you buy a crate engine, sometimes the equipment is included, but in many cases, the controllers must be purchased separately. This engine controller from Chevrolet Performance offers the best of both worlds in a factory-backed computer with performance tuning built in. (Photo Courtesy General Motors)

For a simple aftermarket solution that does not require advanced tuning skills, the FAST EZ-EFI is an easy-to-use system that comes with all the wiring required to control the engine. It does not control the transmission, but it is compatible with TCI transmission controllers. (Photo Courtesy FAST)

systems have some user controls. The Holley HP EFI ECM can be manually tuned in addition to the self-learn function. Where these entry and mid-level systems drop off is in the boost department. When you start adding superchargers or turbos, these controllers may not be compatible; some are, some are not. Just keep that in mind when making your purchase decision.

Although most aftermarket controllers are excellent in terms of engine management, most do not have transmission control for late-model electronic transmissions. Some, such as the Holley Dominator ECM, feature the most advanced tuning capability in the Holley line and a built-in transmission controller. Others require a separate transmission controller. Several aftermarket transmission controllers, such as the TCI version and Painless Performance's Perfect Torc, give you greater tuning capability of the GM electronically controlled transmission than the factory controller.

These units are compatible with most GM electronically controlled automatic transmissions. They provide load, gear, RPM, and speed-based programming with the click of a mouse. The TCI unit also is fully compatible with CAN 2.0B engine management systems such as the FAST XFI system, which makes it easy to integrate the TCU with the engine controller. Transmission controllers come with tuning software and wiring harnesses. The software allows you to change many parameters, even allowing paddle and push-button shifting configurations and manifold-pressure-based shift firmness, greatly adding to the ability to tune the transmission far beyond the capabilities of the stock TCM or ECM.

This carbureted intake and controller from Edelbrock comes with a controller from MSD that mounts directly to the intake, eliminating mounting issues.

This means automatic changes as the environment around the vehicle changes.

Let's say you take a trip across the country. With a static tune, the engine runs differently at different elevations. With self-learning, the tune adapts to the environment much better than a static-tuned ECM. Once the engine is running, the ECM starts learning, so within just a few miles it begins to tune the engine automatically. This means less time working on a laptop trying to get your engine running at its best and more time enjoying the drive. FAST's EZ-EFI and Holley's HP EFI systems both feature self-learn, and they are reliable controllers for LS-series EFI systems.

If you want more control, you can take it. Even the basic self-learn

Performance Project: Installing an Aftermarket Transmission Controller

Unlike the earlier "slushbox" automatic transmissions that soaked up massive amounts of power and left you with sloppy shifts and slower ETs, the modern electronically controlled transmissions operate with much tighter parameters. Considering that 0–60 times for most high-performance vehicles are now spec'd with automatics instead of their manual-shift counterparts, the reality is that the automatic transmission is the better solution. That also means that you need an electronic control unit.

For LS swaps, this is often taken care of when you use a factory ECM, as most of them have the transmission controller built in. If you use an aftermarket controller, carbureted LS, or one of the new LT-series engines, or if you simply want better control of your automatic transmission, you need a separate controller. Yes, you read that correctly: The LT-series engine ECM does not have transmission controls built in; it is a separate controller. A laptop is required for tuning the controller.

Painless Performance has the solution for all these situations; it is called Perfect Torc. Designed to manage GM 4LXX transmissions 1995–up (1995–up 4L80, 1996–up 4L60), this little unit packs a lot of features. Not only does it give you tuning control of the transmission, including shift timing and firmness, it also comes with push buttons for paddle-shifting. For the most basic installation, only four wires must be connected: ignition (handles all power functions), two grounds, and the TPS input. The rest of the wires are secondary controls, including button-shift, speedometer output, and a 5-volt TPS power feed for vehicles that require a standalone TPS unit (carbureted engines). The other wires are bundled together and plug directly into the ports on the transmission.

The installation is quite simple. Under the vehicle, route the transmission harness to the passenger's side of the transmission case. Plug the large round plug into the port on the shelf of the case. A second two-wire plug connects to the rear speed sensor port. Make sure that the wires are routed away from the exhaust and driveshaft. The main harness is long enough to reach the firewall and into the vehicle for most cars and trucks. You could also run the harness through the floor, just be sure to use a grommet to protect the wires from chaffing. This harness has three separate molex connectors. The controller itself should be mounted inside the vehicle (the glovebox or center console are great locations) because it has a diagnostic and tuning function for on-the-fly tests and tuning.

The controller harness has eight wires in one molex connector. These are the power, grounds, sensors, and shift-button wires. As previously stated, only four wires are required for operation. The power wire terminates to a 12-volt source when the ignition is on. This must have power only when the ignition switch is in the run/start position. The ignition switch is the best source for this wire.

The grounds must be terminated as close to the ECM ground as possible. Most LS-engine harnesses have multiple ground points, so locate the closest set and run the ground wires to that point. On the vehicle, the grounds were made to the driver-side valvecover with the ECM grounds; this was directly in front of the large factory grommet in the center of the firewall.

The TPS signal wire can be tricky. If you do not have a pinout for your ECM, you need to trace this wire. This install uses an LT1 ECM. According to the GM ECM wiring diagram (see Chapter 6), port 70 on the C2 or J2 plug is the TPS signal. LS engines typically have two TPS signals (redundant systems); connect to the actual signal side. You can check this with a voltmeter; the wire that changes voltage when moving the throttle open and closed is the correct signal wire.

If you do not have a TPS, you must install one for carbureted LS swaps, so you need to purchase a TPS unit and bracket. The sensor should be labeled with the proper terminals, but the Perfect Torc install manual outlines the procedure for determining the ports of unknown function to get the TPS wired correctly. The harness for the Perfect Torc includes the ground, signal, and 5-volt feed wires required for connection.

The speedometer output can be calibrated to operate any electronic speedometer. All the calibrations are managed in the laptop software that is included with the system. Mechanical speedometers are not supported by GM 4LXX transmissions. If you must retain the mechanical speedometer, an electric-to-mechanical conversion unit is required. The vehicle speed calibration can be done with a GPS unit, with a pace vehicle, or through an adjustable speedometer.

If you want to install a paddle shifter in your vehicle, two wires on the harness are for that purpose. Several push buttons come with the kit for dash or console mounting, or you can purchase a steering wheel adapter with paddles. Three buttons are required. One is wired to each shift wire (turns on/off manual mode), and then each shift wire is connected to a separate switch for shifting. The other side of the up/down button goes to ground. Each press of the button shifts the transmission up or down one gear.

The last wire on the controller harness is for shift table selection. The Perfect Torc unit can manage two tables, allowing the user to set up a performance mode and a race mode, or street and off-road. This uses a toggle switch (included): When this wire is grounded, table 2 is used, when open, table 1 is used. Although not required, this is very useful for dual-purpose vehicles.

Once the wiring is completed, you simply plug in your laptop and run the software. The program has several base tunes that you can choose from and then tweak from there. Load your tables, tune, and then enjoy your freshly tuned transmission.

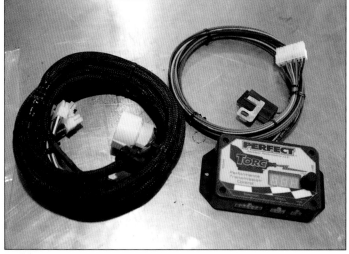

1 *When performing a swap project, you need a transmission controller in the ECM to run and control an automatic transmission. The Perfect Torc from Painless Performance does the job and is simple to install.*

2 *The transmission harness and the module harness are the two major harnesses for the LS engine. The transmission harness routes under the vehicle to the transmission. The main bulkhead plugs into the port on the top of the pan on the passenger's side.*

3 *The tailshaft VSS plugs into the harness on the passenger's side of the tailshaft. Make sure that the wires are routed away from the exhaust and any moving parts. The transmission harness runs into the vehicle through a factory hole in the firewall.*

4 *Inside the car you need to connect several wires. This bundle includes the optional wires for bump shifting and speedometer output. I can use these later, but they are not necessary for the initial install.*

5 *Because the transmission controller keeps the unit working, I opted to solder the power connection. You could crimp it, but if the crimp fails, your transmission can fail too.*

6 *The Perfect Torc needs a TPS signal to function properly. I used the GM wiring guide to locate the TPS signal wire inside the main engine harness.*

7 *To verify I had the right wire, I checked the TPS plug and found the same-color-coded wire.*

8 *Using a pair of auto-strippers, I stripped a 3/4-inch section of the wire. I used a razor blade to remove the stripped insulation completely.*

9 *Next, I had to verify the integrity of the system. Therefore, I put a test wire into the TPS signal port and touched one lead for a multi-meter set on continuity.*

10 *As a precaution to make 100-percent sure you have the right wire, touch the other lead to the stripped wire.*

11 *The trick to soldering a second wire into the middle of another is to split the continuous wire and slide the new wire between the two.*

12 *Wrap the wire around the continuous wire and solder. Wrapping the joint with electrical tape completes the splice.*

13 *I reinstalled the wire loom and taped up the joint where the new TPS signal wire exited the loom. I used Painless' Power Braid to conceal the signal wire.*

14 *The Perfect Torc system uses two ground wires, which must be grounded close to the ECM ground. I secured the one pair of ECM grounds (there are two pairs total for the LT1 ECM) and both Perfect Torc grounds to the rearmost driver-side valvecover bolt.*

FUEL SYSTEM

Installing a fuel-injection system on a classic muscle car that was originally equipped with a carbureted fuel system requires careful planning and component selection. Many components that go into a fuel system, including the tank, fuel pump, lines, fittings, and filters, must be replaced or upgraded. Simply installing an electric fuel pump does not work. The fuel-pressure requirements alone necessitate detailed planning, including pressure regulator, filtration, and line sizing.

Fuel Pumps

You have the choice of an in-tank or externally mounted fuel pump. Most owners opt for the in-tank pump because of improved performance and reliability. In-tank pumps are more complicated to install, but tend to last longer, hold higher pressure, and are quieter. You need to detach the tank from the chassis before installing the pump and sending unit in it, or you could buy a complete aftermarket tank. Virtually any aftermarket EFI in-tank pump can supply the 60-psi fuel pressure required. Many builders recommend the Walbro 340 in-tank pump because it holds higher pressures and provides excellent performance for LS engines. Many in-tank pumps are available. The key is to buy a pump that is suited for your application. The stock F-Body fuel pump assembly can be purchased from GM dealers and used for retrofits.

When opting for an in-tank pump, you need to either buy a

A replacement tank is an alternative to dealing with crusty old stock sending units. An Aeromotive Phantom fuel pump has been installed in this Tanks replacement fuel tank. It's a simple process to bolt in and wire up the pump.

When the pump cavitates, several problems and damage are the result. Part A shows a typical off-brand filter; the small sintered metal filter restricts flow to the pump. Part B shows the actual damage inside the pump. Cavitation grooves the aluminum and metal shavings enter the system and ruin the pump. (Photo Courtesy Aeromotive Inc.)

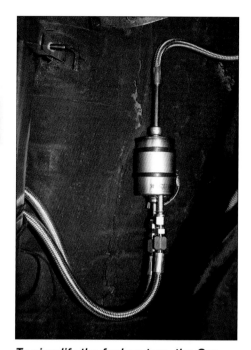

The pump is located in a recess in the center of the tank. This means that the tank fits flush just like the factory tank without any modifications to the car. A 0- to 90-ohm fuel level sender is included as well.

I recommend prewiring the pump and installing the hose fittings because once the tank has been installed, you do not have much room to do it.

To simplify the fuel system, the Corvette regulator-filter is bypassed by adding a full-length return line under your car. The regulator-filter keeps the fuel pressure at 67 psi and redirects the unused fuel back to the tank.

Unlike the factory tank, the new unit has a detachable filler neck, so it doesn't look stock. It also makes the tank easier to install and remove. The neck does require support at the bumper, which must be fabricated.

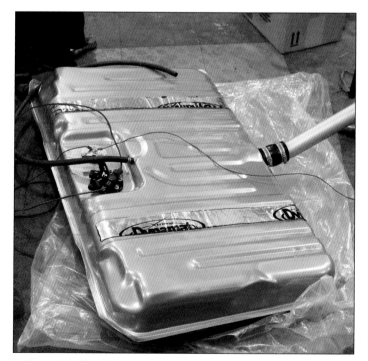

I also added strips of sound deadener on top of the tank. The factory tank has rubber/asphalt strips, which do not come with the new tank. This stuff is much better anyway.

The tank installs using the original straps in the original location.

tank with a preinstalled EFI pump or install the pump in the existing tank. Both options can be pricey, but there are ways to keep it on the cheap as well. New tanks can cost upwards of $1,000. Companies such as Aeromotive build custom stainless steel gas tanks with built-in in-tank pumps. These tanks are well-built and easy to install. Each Aeromotive Phantom EFI fuel tank features a dropped sump in the top of the tank. This allows for adequate floor clearance. Each EFI tank comes with a new high-volume high-pressure fuel pump to feed the LS engine. The A-Body tank is a drop-in fit.

Ambitious builders can choose to modify the stock tank themselves. Note that the following procedure requires welding on a gas tank. Serious injury or death can occur if the utmost care and preparations are not followed.

You can alter your stock tank to take an EFI fuel pump in three ways. The bargain-basement method is to take the stock sending unit assembly out of the tank, cut off a short section of feed line (about 1½ inches, depending on the depth of the tank and the length of the pump), and fit the pump to the stub using fuel line and hose clamps. The important thing here is to make sure the pump is mounted about 1/4 inch off the floor of the tank with a filter sock resting on the bottom of the tank. This keeps impurities out of the pump while getting the most fuel out of the tank.

The pump must be supported; a piece of steel rod can be welded to the underside of the assembly plate. The pump is then clamped to the rod so it remains stationary. This method doesn't work for all tanks, especially shallow tanks, and you may be ham-

Holley has a version of an in-tank pump. This one uses hydramat technology to eliminate the need for a baffle; the hydramat soaks up fuel at any angle as long as it is touching it. (Photo Courtesy Holley Performance Products)

pered by the diameter of the stock assembly. Also, the fuel-level sending unit may be in the way, depending on the application. This method keeps the stock feed lines in place and eliminates floorpan clearance issues. One drawback is the lack of a fuel sump, which traps fuel around the pump inlet, ensuring it does not run dry. Running an in-tank pump dry is very destructive; they don't last long when run dry.

The second option involves welding on the tank. This is extremely dangerous and should not be attempted in haste or by novices. *All* old fuel must be removed, and the tank thoroughly rinsed, drained, and rinsed again until there is absolutely no possibility of any remaining fuel vapor. If you smell a hint of gas, do it again. To add an extra measure of safety, fill the tank with water or inert gas such as argon while the welding is being performed. If you have any doubt, seek the help of a professional. Most fuel tank builders offer their services for retrofitting tanks. Employ their services if you can.

Installing a custom in-tank pump in the top of the tank often requires a recessed panel on the top. The fittings clear the floorpan and give you a flat surface to mount the new

assembly. If you place the top sump to the side of the original, the stock sending unit can be used, simplifying the process. This requires a boxed section be built and welded to the top of the tank. Then a fuel-pump assembly unit is built with both wiring and inlet and outlet fittings. This piece should have a bar or rod on the inside portion of the tank for the pump to mount to.

Using 90-degree hose barb fittings is usually the easiest way to get the fuel in and out of the assembly. These fittings must be sealed tight so they do not leak. The entire assembly bolts to the sump.

In addition, by installing baffles to the inside of the tank, fuel surrounds the pump at all times. These should be added before the top sump is installed.

You can also weld in a sump in the bottom of the tank. This sump is placed directly below the pump, but the pump is installed in the lowered section, with the filter sock on the floor of the sump. Tanksinc.com offers an upper tank mount, complete with a fuel pump and baffle. This reduces some of the legwork in building this piece and ensures the pump always is covered with fuel.

The third option allows you to install a truly high-performance fuel pump into a stock fuel tank without welding. Aeromotive offers two retrofit in-tank pump kits: the Phantom and the A1000 Stealth. For basic street performance use, the Phantom 340 is suitable. This kit allows you to simply cut a hole in the top of the tank, drop in the pump, bolt it down, and hook up the lines. The kit comes with the seals, hardware, and a drill jig to ensure the holes are in the right place. The 340 supports up to 700-hp supercharged EFI engines, or 1,000-hp supercharged carbureted systems. That leaves plenty of room to power a stock 400 LS3. The Phantom system fits in just about any tank, so this is a good option that takes out the guesswork.

For more serious performance engines, the Stealth A1000 system feeds up to 1,300-hp EFI systems and 1,500 for carbureted engines. Installing these systems takes slightly more effort than the Phantom kit, but not much.

Inline Fuel Pumps

External or inline pumps offer a simpler installation and are usually more affordable, so you can make roadside swaps. The main gripe over inline pumps is the noise. The relatively quiet and smooth-running Gen III/IV engines do not drown out many external sounds, including these inline pumps. Therefore, drivers may hear the whir of the electric pump sound over the engine with a stock-style quiet exhaust. For most builders, the added noise isn't a problem but rather an inconvenience, but for a show car, a noisy pump might be considered a serious drawback.

The real drawback for an inline pump is that the fuel line is only pressurized after the pump, so the tank to the pump is gravity fed. Anyone who has dealt with a modern high-performance external fuel pump can tell you that life is difficult when you lose the siphon in the tank. Simply having the pump in the tank maintains a constant supply of fuel to prevent those hard-cornering and acceleration woes that come with a stock tank and an inline electric fuel pump. Inline fuel pumps also require a more substantial return line system because of the long distance between the regulator and the fuel tank. Inline pumps are also subject to failure through heat. The only thing that cools the pump is the gas flowing through it.

Not all inline pumps are created equal. External pumps come in all different shapes and sizes, with most of the market consisting of low-pressure units designed for carburetors. These pumps deliver 6 to 14 psi, and are not close to the 60 psi required to operate an LS engine. Any less than 60 psi and it leans out and does not run well, if at all. You have plenty of inline EFI pump choices. Many builders prefer the Walbro GSL 392 external pump. These pumps are well-suited for Gen III/IV engines and can supply the pressure needed.

Installing an inline pump is simple, but there are a few caveats. The first is to *always* install a pre-filter before the pump, so the pump does not become clogged and ruined. A pre-filter is basically a screen-style filter that traps the big stuff. A micron filter should be placed after the pump to catch small contaminants. Do not install a micron filter in front of the pump (between the tank and the pump) because it impedes the gravity feed and there is not enough force to push the fuel through a micron filter.

Make sure the pre-filter is large enough to free-flow the fuel. A small pre-filter restricts flow to the pump, causing cavitation, and burns up the pump. A stock-type metal canister pre-filter works great, but they are not pretty. Most aftermarket fuel pump makers have large-capacity pre-filters if you want one that looks good. Most of the aftermarket pre-filters are rebuildable as well.

Cavitation is a natural process that occurs when vapor bubbles are induced in liquid under pressure. All electric fuel pumps are susceptible to this force. Its most common cause is installer error when an inadequate fuel supply increases the suction on the inlet side. Cavitation is literally boiling the fuel through pressure. Vapor bubbles form and then split, imploding, causing a micro explosion. This is extremely damaging; even a few minutes of cavitation can ruin a fuel pump.

Another cause of cavitation is overheated fuel. Not running a return line (deadhead style) or attempting to plumb the return line into the feed line (not into the tank) causes hot fuel to cycle back through the pump, heating it up more. The hotter the fuel, the easier it is to cavitate or even vapor lock. Yes, EFI systems can vapor lock too. This is the reason a proper return system is so important for EFI.

The most important aspect of any electric fuel pump is the wiring. It is most difficult to get solid grounds because paint, rust, and scale inhibit the ground. Always be sure to remove the paint and anything else from the ground location, so you have clean metal. Electricity requires equal grounding and positive current flow. A bad ground is just as bad as a faulty positive feed. Electric fuel pumps require a lot of current; running a relay circuit from the pump trigger lead, along with 12-gauge positive and negative wires to the fuel pump, provides ample capacity. This ensures the pump receives the required amperage without overheating the wires. Do not run a

16-to-24-gauge primary wire to a fuel pump because it will cause a fire. All fuel pumps require at least 12-gauge power wire, with the larger pumps needing 10-gauge wire. This includes both power and ground wires.

Gen V LT-series engines are different from the LS series, particularly in the fuel system department. All LT-series engines are direct-injection,

meaning the fuel is pressurized to more than 2,000 psi and injected directly into the combustion chamber, much like a diesel engine. Because of this, the fuel system is dramatically different. Instead of a basic fuel pump and regulator, the factory pump is controlled by the ECM and a fuel pump module to control the pressure.

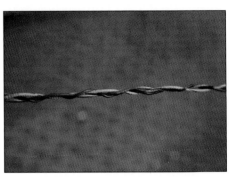

LT-series engines use a different style of fuel feed. Instead of the standard return line, the direct-injection fuel system uses a pulse width modulation (PWM) controlled pump that varies the pump speed to maintain 72 psi. This little computer and sensor manages that operation.

The PWM signal is highly susceptible to inference. To remedy that, the wires are twisted or braided. The harnesses in the GM ECM kit are not long enough to reach the back of an A-Body, so you extend their length. A minimum of 27 twists per 8 feet is required. I lightly braided mine to keep it from untwisting.

To add the pressure sensor, I needed a fuel log. Buying one is easy, but I had some leftover fuel rail and made one. The sensor has 10-mm metric threads, and adapting that to an existing log is difficult, so this works best.

First, I drilled into the center of the block until I hit the port.

Next, I stepped up to the correct bit size for the threads on the adapter. I have a small -6 AN to 10-mm adapter; it is a brake fitting.
Then I secured the block in a bench vise, and used a high-quality tap to cut a 9/16-inch threaded hole in the block. Use cutting fluid or lubricant to keep the tap from galling in the block.

The adapter port has been finished and is ready for installation. This 3-inch-long block from Holley includes a section of universal fuel rail for direct-port EFI kits.

I tapped the ends for -6 O-ring fittings, and then installed the proper fittings and sensor with O-rings and thread sealant.

Here is the adapter fitting. It is -6 male on one side and 10-mm male on the other. These are hard to find; you have to order them online.

I installed an Aeromotive post-filter (100-micron filtration) to the sensor block. This filters the fuel after the sensor before it gets to the engine.

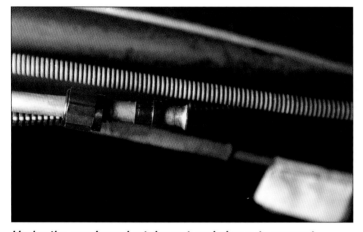

Under the car, I used a tube nut and sleeve to convert the 3/8-inch feed line to mate with the -6 AN fittings. This reduces the potential for leaks and AN fittings seal very well.

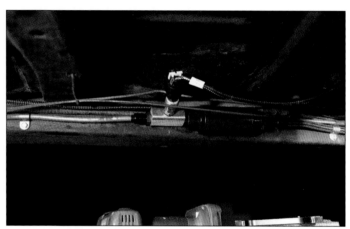

I connected each line to the block and filter assembly and secured the lines with bolt-in clamps. Make sure the wires for the sensor are routed away from heat and moving objects.

I mounted the fuel controller between the floorpan and transmission cross-member. This is as far back as the harness allows. The controller is weatherproof. Just make sure that the plug is flat or pointed downward; do not position the plug where water can accumulate. This mounting also limits the potential for debris damage.

A special pressure sensor in the fuel line monitors the pressure of the fuel, which is maintained at 72 psi. Rather than use a regulator, the pressure is managed through PWM control of the pump. Essentially, the ECM uses PWM to control the speed of the pump, ensuring constant full pressure with no delays. This complicates the fuel system for the LT-series engine swap. You can't use just any pump; the pump has to be able to be PWM controlled. Before you purchase a pump, make sure it is PWM capable.

The LT system is returnless to keep the fuel temperature down; therefore, hot fuel does not return to the tank and the fuel temperature stays down. The pump requirements are 72 psi at 45 gallons per hour (gph) with the Chevrolet Performance control system. Although this system is more complicated in terms of wiring, it does eliminate the need for a return line.

Many swappers already have an existing electronic fuel system in their vehicle. Swapping an LT into that scenario could mean buying new parts, but all is not lost. You can bypass the PWM-style pump system by using a standard electric pump with a return line and regulator set to 72 psi at 45 gph. That is fairly high for a street pump, so make sure your pump is capable of providing the required flow and pressure.

Installing the PWM controller is relatively simple, but installing the fuel pressure sensor is a bit difficult. First, you need an inline adapter with a pressure sensor port positioned at 90 degrees, or 5 to 85 degrees to the flow of fuel, according to the GM manual for the fuel controller. Because plenty of these fuel sensor adapters are available, this is relatively easy.

The problem is that most of the adapters are for 1/8-inch NPT fittings, and not the 10-mm threads required for the GM sensor. Finding a 1/8-inch NPT male to 10-mm male adapter is the difficult part. What you can find easily is a -6 AN male to 10-mm adapter. To use this, you need an aluminum fuel log or Y-block fuel splitter and a -6 AN to 10-mm male-male adapter. This allows you to connect the sensor into the fuel system. (I made one with a leftover piece of fuel rail from another project.)

The PWM pump controller is a plug-and-play component, but the pump wiring is not. Three wires come off the pump module: yellow with a black stripe, gray, and a smaller-gauge black wire. The yellow/black wire is the ground, the gray wire is the power side, and the small black wire is the shield. If you have a GM pump with a shield pin, connect the small black wire to that pin; if you have a pump without a shield pin, leave the wire unterminated and tape it to the other wires.

Because of the nature of PWM control, you may experience electromagnetic interference from other electronics in the car. To keep this from interrupting the control signal, the two main power control wires are twisted with a third shielding wire. This wire is grounded to the chassis near the pump. The Chevrolet Performance wiring harness comes with a certain length only; the A-Body chassis absolutely requires longer wires. To maintain the shielding, you must twist the wires a minimum of 27 twists per 8 feet of wire.

The best way to ensure that the wires are correctly twisted and don't unravel is to braid the three wires together. It does not need to be a tight braid, rather a consistent loose braid, wrapping the wires around every 3 inches or so. Do not use crimp connectors for these wires; make sure you solder them well and use shrink tubing.

Most EFI engines (except for 2014–up Gen V LT-series engines) require return lines. This can sometimes be confusing because Gen III/IV engines use a single-line fuel rail. The 1997–1998 Corvettes and 1998–2002 F-Body LS1s used a dual-line fuel rail. In 1999, the Corvette LS1 went to a single-line rail, using a

The stock fuel rails use a snap-on clip fitting. I used these fittings because they convert the GM clip-on style to -6 AN fittings for a clean look.

The adapter pops on and the clip keeps it secured in place. This is very convenient and makes servicing the fuel system easier because the clips can be a pain to remove.

LS engines need a return line, and it also connects using the push-on fittings. Most 1970–1972 A-Body cars have a factory hard line that runs back to the tank (5/16 inch), so you can simply connect to that line. If you don't have one, you need to run one. It can be a regular fuel line because the return side is low pressure.

It is a good idea to pressure test the fuel system before firing up the engine. This helps you find any leaks and address them before the situation becomes dangerous. LS engines require 60 psi to operate.

filter regulator near the fuel tank and running a short return line back to the tank. This configuration is much simpler and requires only a single line run the length of the vehicle. Many builders prefer to run two lines the distance of the vehicle with the dual-line fuel rails.

The benefit of running a full-length return system is cooler fuel. The fuel does not sit in the lines, heating up from the pressure. Instead, a constant flow of fuel is running through the lines, ensuring cooler fuel and, therefore, more power. This, of course, requires two sets of fuel lines: a 3/8-inch line for the feed and a 5/16-inch line for the return. Some muscle cars and trucks came with return-style mechanical pump fuel systems, but these are not the norm for older vehicles; most were deadhead systems, meaning that the fuel simply stops at the pump until it is sent on to the engine.

If you choose the simple one-line route, you need the 1999-up Corvette filter regulator. This unit has two lines (an input and an output): one on the side for the fuel tank, and one on the other side for the output, which goes to the engine. It is a one-line system to the engine, and there is a short return line from the regulator/filter to the tank. This pre-set regulator provides the correct 60 psi to the engine, which pressurizes the entire fuel line while pumping the excess fuel back to the tank. This is typically mounted as close to the tank as possible to minimize the length of feed and return lines to the tank.

For a dual-line system with the pump in the tank, you need a filter between the pump and the fuel rails. It is best to filter the fuel as soon as possible to keep the fuel lines as clean as possible.

Installing new lines is not difficult, but it can be nerve racking. You have three ways to accomplish this task: install pre-bent hard lines, bend new hard lines, or run braided hose,. Using pre-bent hard lines is the simplest method if the vehicle has the fuel tank in the stock location. Pre-bent lines such as those from Classic Tube and Tube Tech are patterned after the original lines in the car and should fit just like the originals. That is not to say that compromises and tweaks are not needed along the way.

Bending and installing custom lines most effectively transports fuel the length of the vehicle, but it is much easier said than done. This is a challenging task that requires some metalworking skills, and therefore the task is frustrating at best for the novice. Tube manufacturers such as Classic Tube offer custom bending services. Using coat hangers or other wire, a pattern is bent by hand and sent to the maker. The maker bends a set of hard lines to your specifications and ships it to you. This ensures quality bends with proper flare where you want them (without kinks) and without the aggravation of doing it yourself.

The third option is to use flexible hose for the long runs. This works, but you should use braided hose rather than plain rubber hose to protect from road debris damage. The chance of road debris snagging a long braided fuel line is much higher than with a hard line. Rubber lines are not the best option, either. Rubber lines dry out and crack much faster than hard lines corrode, so you must replace the rubber lines eventually.

Performance Project: Installing a Phantom Pump System

Until recently, installing an in-tank fuel pump meant buying a custom tank or doing a lot of dangerous cutting and welding on your tank. Thanks to some ingenuity from Aeromotive, that is no longer the case. The Phantom-series of in-tank pumps allows you to quickly, easily, and safely install an in-tank pump into most stock fuel tanks. The GM A-Body tank is a bit problematic when it comes to this install; there is only one good place to locate the pump, so you have to be careful when setting it up.

The main issue with the Phantom system is that it needs a fairly flat surface to be installed. Aeromotive knows that most tanks are corrugated. You can install the system on uneven surfaces up to 1/4 inch deep, by way of the included high-density rubber gasket. The A-Body tank has deep ribs, so on 1969 and older tanks, the front passenger's side is really about the only location you can use. Depending on the model of vehicle, there may or may not be vents at that location. The vent tube runs the length of the tank, so it must be removed and plugged. There are some variances in the A-Body tanks by make, model, and year, so plan accordingly.

Before starting this process, make sure the tank is empty of fuel. It is a good idea to rinse it out with water and dry it with compressed air to remove any fuel vapors.

Once you have chosen the install location, it's time to cut. I used a 3¼-inch hole saw to make the hole. Go slow and take your time. Most of the metal shaving stays outside the tank, but you end up with some inside. That is okay because you should vacuum it out later anyway. The kit comes with the necessary drill jig that fits perfectly inside the 3¼-inch hole.

Place the jig in the hole; make sure none of the drill holes run through the angled section of any corrugations in the tank. The mounting studs must be through flat metal. Drill two holes opposite each other, and then use the supplied bolts and nuts to secure the jig in the tank. Once secure, drill the rest of the holes and remove the jig. At this point, you should clean the tank with a vacuum to remove any metal shavings.

Measure the tank depth and add 1 inch. Cut the foam baffle to that length. You want it a little longer than the tank to keep it in place. The kit comes with a stud ring; this installs from the inside of the tank. It is split on one side to go into the hole. Install this and pull the studs through the sheet metal. Drop the drill jig over the studs and loosely thread a couple of nuts onto the studs to hold it in place. Press the baffle through the hole and position the foam around the stud ring.

Using the tank depth measurement, assemble the pump and filter sock and set the max depth to be the same as the tank depth. Cut the pump mounting arm to accommodate this depth. It is critical that the pump sock sit on the bottom of the tank; otherwise you can starve the pump for fuel, which kills it. Cut the supplied fuel hose to match the installed depth and assemble the pump to the housing using the clamps provided. Don't forget to install the wiring harness.

Slip the gasket into the pump assembly, remove the drill jig, slide the pump into the tank, and drop the housing over the studs on the ring. Thread the nuts and washers onto the studs and tighten them in a crisscross pattern evenly to seat the housing and not dis-tort or break the studs. You can overtighten the studs and break them, so be careful. Hand tight is all you need; don't use an impact.

Now the tank can be installed in the vehicle. For A-Body cars, space the tank down about 1/2 inch to achieve clearance for the pump assembly. You can do this with foam or wood blocks, or fabricate two metal wedges. Another option is to cut or dimple the trunk pan over the housing.

With the tank installed, you can wire it up and run the lines. This system is capable of return or returnless plumbing and can be PWM controlled for LT-series or aftermarket ECM control. The housing uses -6 fittings with 3/8-inch hard fuel lines, making it perfect for factory or aftermarket fuel line.

1 *Each Phantom fuel system comes with baffle, pump, install ring, and all related hardware. They install easily into the A-Body tank.*

2 *I started by cleaning the tank and marking the location for the pump. There is really only one suitable spot, the front passenger's corner.*

3 *Drill the tank for the center of the mounting hole. I pre-drilled this because hole saws have a bad habit of breaking or jerking your hand when you go through the metal and the blade catches on the steel. Always practice safe drilling.*

4 *Cut the hole using the correct-size hole saw. A good quality bi-metal saw is necessary.*

5 *Inside the tank is a long vent tube. Some A-Body tanks have this, some have just a short port. Remove the line if it is in the way.*

6 *To fill the hole, run a 1/4-20 tap through the hole.*

7 *Add some high-strength threadlocking compound to a stainless-steel bolt and thread it into the hole.*

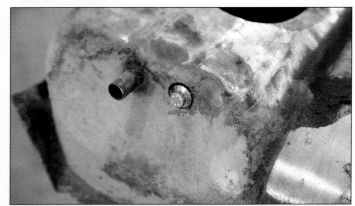

8 *Add a nut and washer on the inside of the tank to help seal the hole. It won't leak now.*

9 *Place the drill jig into the hole and align it so that the holes are not in the side of a rib (very important), and drill two opposing holes.*

10 *Place a single bolt into one of the two holes to secure the jig in place and keep it from twisting while drilling the remaining holes.*

11 *Measure the tank at the bottom and cut the foam baffle 1 inch longer than the total depth. A razor blade or serrated knife is the easiest way to cut the foam.*

12 *Place the baffle inside the tank. You must fold it onto itself, but it conforms relatively easily.*

13 *To secure the pump housing, place the split ring into the tank, align the studs, and press it up through the holes previously drilled.*

14 *The studs should be fully exposed. The foam baffle goes around the outside of the ring.*

15 *The pump gets a filter sock and the rubber sleeve slides over the pump body.*

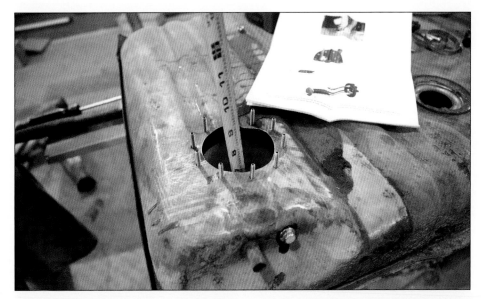

16 *Measure the tank depth again, this time for the pump depth.*

17 *Transfer that measurement to the pump housing and position the pump to touch the bottom of the tank. An A-Body tank should measure 7 inches, but it is critical that you measure it on your tank for absolute certainty.*

18 Cut the rail a little short so that it does not impede the placement of the pump. A hacksaw makes quick work of the bracket. One notch short is suitable.

19 This pump is being used with the LT1 PWM system, so I drill a 1/32-inch hole drilled into the brass plug. This is a pressure vent and is only required for PWM returnless usage. This pump works great for return systems without this modification.

20 Secure the pump to the housing and the fuel line to the top with band clamps. The wiring simply plugs in.

21 A foam pad goes onto the top of the studs and then the pump housing drops into the tank. Be careful not to pinch the wires.

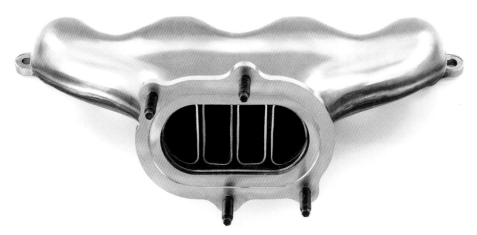

These LS7 flanges differ from the classic Chevy three-bolt flange. You may need a long section of the downpipes to ensure you include the flange. Center-dump manifolds may or may not clear the A-Body chassis, depending on the adapter mounts. (Photo Courtesy General Motors)

install and not fit another. Test fitting is the only way to verify fit.

Stock exhaust manifolds also need a compatible flange that can be welded to the rest of the exhaust system. Several flanges are used on stock exhaust manifolds, but not all of them are reproduced. The trick here is to make sure you include some of the stock exhaust, the section just below the flange, so that you have the right flanges for the exhaust manifolds. If the flange is not available, fabrication is the only option.

Speedway Motors reproduces exhaust flanges for the LS1 and Vortec manifolds. Another source for flanges is used catalytic converters. You can't buy a used converter, but you can buy the flanges. Most salvage yards will gladly cut them off and sell them to you.

Using the exhaust gasket as a pattern, you can cut a flange using a plasma cutter. An acetylene torch certainly cuts the steel, but it's not the correct tool for this job because it also warps it to the point that it isn't usable for an exhaust flange. Depending on your install, there are a couple of ways to cut new flanges.

The most common material for flanges is mild steel. For a good seal, material of 1/8 inch or thicker should be used. With a good basic outer dimension measured from the manifold or exhaust gasket, your local metal supply shop should be able to provide a plate cut to fit. Depending on the shop, they may be able to cut

The stock manifolds may or may not fit your application; information on stock manifold fitment is sketchy at best. Truck manifolds are usually too big to clear the firewall in most muscle cars, but that also depends on the forward placement. Swap headers are readily available and fit much better.

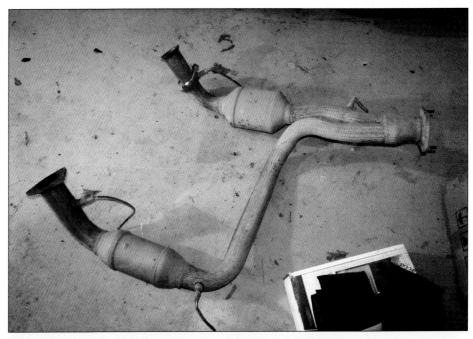

Stock downpipes also usually have catalytic converters. If you need to use them, it will save you some cash down the road. Upgrading to a high-flow cat frees up some horsepower; the choice is yours.

out the entire part for you. Otherwise, using the basic plates, you can trace the inside of the gasket to the plate and then, using a plasma cutter, trim out the plate to the outside edge of the line. Any metal overhang can cause some turbulence in the airflow, which impedes flow and reduces horsepower but does not significantly affect performance if the overhang is small.

If you do not have access to a plasma cutter, the following procedure allows you to remove any metal overhang. Using a drill bit, drill to the line at some point. If you are using Z06 manifolds, do this in each corner. Then place the flange in a vice and use a reciprocating saw, air body saw, or hacksaw to cut out the center section. It may take a while, but it works. A plasma cutter, of course, certainly makes the quickest work of the job.

An aluminum flange looks great with stainless, chrome, or polished exhausts. Cutting aluminum is easier than cutting steel and a good-looking set of aluminum flanges could be cut from plate aluminum with a band saw and a scroll saw quite easily. Aluminum is softer than steel, so the aluminum flanges must be thicker than their steel counterparts. Aluminum flanges should be made from at least 1/4- or 3/8-inch plate. The cutting process is the same. Plasma torches quickly cut aluminum, so be careful. If you use the hand-cut method, aluminum is softer, making it a little easier. Also, aluminum cleans up nicely with carbide tips and a die grinder.

If your local shop is equipped with a CNC plasma or water jet, you can pay them to cut the parts for you. The cutting part is usually not very expensive, but the program writ-

ing time is typically around $50 per hour. Because the flanges are simple, it shouldn't take a shop longer than an hour. Once the program has been written, a shop can make as many as you want. If you are doing multiple swaps, you can amortize the cost to several engines.

Bridging the gap between a factory manifold fitment and the performance of headers are Hooker cast-iron LS manifolds. These manifolds provide tight fitment coupled with better flow performance and they use 2010 Camaro–type flanges. The manifolds come with the flanges and use the OEM gaskets for a leak-free seal.

2014–Up Gen V LT-Series Manifolds

Currently, the factory offers two types of manifolds for the LT series:

LT1 car manifolds do not fit the A-Body. The truck version may fit, but that has not been verified.

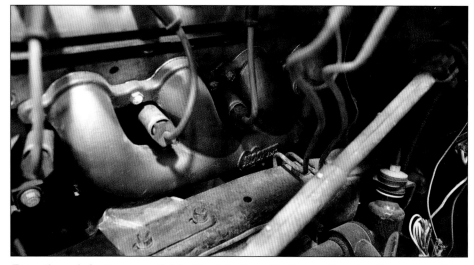

Even though factory manifolds fit a lot of applications, they don't necessarily have the right look. These Hooker LS manifolds fit many applications and come with 2010 Camaro–type flanges for a good seal without searching for parts or gaskets. Although not pictured in an A-Body, they do fit the chassis.

Corvette and truck. The Vette manifolds do not fit the A-Body at all, not even close. The truck manifolds have been reported to fit in some applications, but I have not been able to verify that. Although the flanges are very similar to the LS's, the bolts are in different places, so swapping LS manifolds to the LT is not feasible.

Headers

With all the challenges of modifying stock manifolds, most swappers prefer aftermarket headers designed for engine swaps. Ground clearance is a common concern. Mid-length headers tend to fit best and offer the most ground clearance, but long-tubes certainly work for LS swaps as well. Manufacturers such as Hooker, Edelbrock, and Dynatech custom-fit headers for the most popular LS swap vehicles.

Choosing headers requires careful measurements and research. You need to be careful: Some headers might fit your application but have the stock-style flange, putting you back in the same boat. Sure, you could chop off the stock flange and weld on a new one, but isn't that part of the reason you are buying aftermarket headers? Some vehicle-specific headers fit late-model chassis and are designed for LS engines. These headers do not have the stock-style flange, making them excellent candidates for swap applications.

Vehicle-specific swap headers come with the universal three-bolt triangular flange that has been used for decades. This ensures that the headers easily mate to the rest of the exhaust. Kits are available for specific vehicles that include the headers and exhaust, all in one package.

Edelbrock

This conversion kit includes Edelbrock headers made of 409 stainless steel tubing with 3/8-inch-thick port and collector flanges. The collectors use graphite donut gaskets instead of the leak-prone three-bolt collector and gasket. These fit 1964–1972 GM A-Body cars including the Chevelle, Malibu, El Camino, Cutlass, 442, Skylark, Buick Special, GS350, GS455, GTO, LeMans, and Tempest. The Gen III/IV swap headers have 1¾-inch primary tubes stepped up to 1⅞ inches for maximum flow and power.

Edelbrock recommends using the Edelbrock LS-series engine mount kit (PN 6701) with the Edelbrock swap headers.

For those with Edelbrock E-Tec–series LS heads or Vortec Fast Burn heads, the Edelbrock swap headers (PN 65083) have the correct port flange configuration, so they are compatible with stock A-Body engine mounts.

The Edelbrock LS swap exhaust system matches with the headers and engine mounts, though the system works well with other mounts and headers. The exhaust system is constructed from 2½-inch 409 stainless-steel tubing with an X-pipe assembly and includes a pair of SDT mufflers and a pair of polished stainless-steel tips. This kit fits the same vehicles as the headers.

Hooker

Hooker builds a couple of vehicle-specific LS swap headers: first-generation Camaro and Firebird and GM A-Body, in addition to its universal block hugger LS headers.

The 1966–1972 GM A-Body: These headers are built with lightweight, 18-gauge tuned-length 1¾-inch primaries, with 3-inch smooth-transition slip-fit-style collectors. This yields a leak-free fit to the rest of the exhaust. The headers are designed to fit tight to the chassis, giving increased ground clearance, from 1 to 3 inches, which is especially helpful for lowered vehicles.

The cylinder head flanges are made from 5/16-inch machined steel for a good seal. To accommodate the oxygen sensors, the headers include 3- to 2½-inch slip-fit reducers with oxygen sensor bungs welded in, plus a set of extra bungs for a 3-inch exhaust system.

Hooker LS swap headers fit most manual and automatic GM transmissions, including the Tremec 5- and 6-speed manual transmissions. These headers fit other vehicles as well; research is required. These headers are designed to work with the Hooker LS swap adapters and crossmembers.

Hooker Block Hugger: This LS swap header design is tuned for low- and mid-range street performance from idle to 3,500 rpm. The primaries are made from 18-gauge 1⅝-inch mild steel tubing, which is mandrel bent and tuned by length to reduce back pressure and increase exhaust velocity. This design delivers more power and torque with crisp throttle response; the 2½-inch collectors with a 3/8-inch-thick three-bolt flange make installation simple.

The head flange is machined to ensure a flat surface for a tight seal. The tight-tuck tube design is used to fit within narrow street rod frames and provides a good fit in most vehicles that do not have a dedicated swap header. The collectors exit parallel with the oil pan for maximum ground clearance in lowered vehicles and are positioned to clear the starter and engine mounts.

A starter motor is often not considered during these projects, but it can present a clearance issue with some headers and manifolds. The stock starter (left) is small and powerful, but the new Petronix Contour version (right) is powerful and sculpted to give more clearance for exhaust. Unlike the stock starter, the Contour unit puts all the components inside the case, protecting them from heat and the elements.

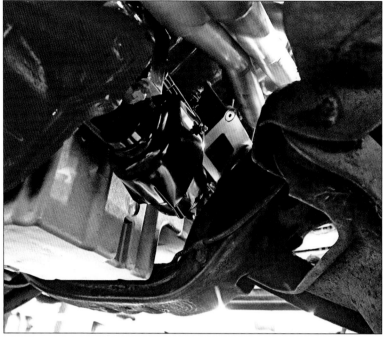

Each starter is also clockable, so it can be rotated to clear obstacles, which makes it perfect for any LS swap.

Doug's Headers

Specifically for A-Body cars, these full-length headers feature 1⅞-inch primaries with a 3-inch collector made from 16-gauge steel and a V-band type of flange for easy leak-free maintenance. They are available in ceramic-coated or natural finish.

2014–up Gen V LT Headers

At press time, no A-Body-specific headers are available for the LT. For the GS shown in this book, I had a set custom made using the LS tube pattern for the A-Body with LT flanges. It is very close, but needs a little tweaking before it is perfect. With that in mind, by the time this book is on the shelf, there should be several LT-compatible options for A-Body swaps. The biggest difference is that the heads are slightly different, so the angle of the flanges must change. I have not tried any headers for trucks or Corvette applications;

some mid-length or shorty-type headers may fit the A-Body.

Catalytic Converters

Your swap project must be equipped with a catalytic converter if the area or state where you license the vehicle mandates and tests vehicles for carbon emissions. You want to choose a catalytic converter that enhances performance yet meets emissions standards. Research on the construction of a catalytic converter will inform your decision.

The most important part is the ceramic matrix. Shaped like a honeycomb, the matrix is made

The catalytic convertor is another key component to the exhaust system. Although many states allow you to swap late-model engines without the hassle of emissions equipment, some states require it. You can use the stock stuff or switch to high-flow aftermarket parts. The core ceramic honeycomb is washed in the oxides and metals to make it function.

predominantly of a ceramic material called cordierite. The honeycomb is created through an extrusion process in which lengths of the honeycomb shape are squeezed through a die and supported by computer-controlled jets of air that keep the honeycomb straight as it leaves the machine.

Once the ceramic honeycomb is fired and set, it receives a washcoat of various oxides combined with the precious metals that function as the actual catalyst. The washcoat is used because it evenly disperses the metals throughout all the pores of the matrix. The metals are generally mixed to best use their individual properties. Most cats in the United States use some combination of platinum, palladium, and rhodium. Outside the United States, copper has been tried, but it forms dioxin, a toxic substance with carcinogenic properties. In some places, materials such as nickel, cerium in washcoat, and manganese in cordierite are used, but each has its disadvantages.

Originally developed throughout the 1930s and 1940s for industrial smoke stacks, catalytic converters began to be developed for automobiles in the 1950s by inventor Eugene Houdry. The first cats were mandated in 1975. They were of a two-way type, which combined oxygen with the carbon monoxide and unburned hydrocarbons to form carbon dioxide and water. As the science progressed, stricter environmental regulations brought about a change to three-way converters in 1981. These more advanced cats also reduce nitrogen oxide.

Catalytic converters work using a redox reaction. This means that once the catalyst is up to operating temperature (from 500 to 1,200 degrees Fahrenheit) both an oxidation reaction and reduction reaction occur simultaneously. That sounds a little complicated, but it just means that molecules are simultaneously losing and gaining electrons. These types of reactions are extremely common; photosynthesis and rust are both good examples of redox reactions.

In the first stage of the catalytic converter, the reduction stage, the goal is to remove the nitrous oxide and especially the nitric oxide, which when introduced to air quickly changes into nitrogen dioxide, which is very poisonous. The reduction stage works because the nitrogen molecule in the nitrogen oxide wants to bond much more strongly with the metals of the catalyst than it does with its oxygen molecules and the oxygen molecules would rather bond with each other, forming oxygen, which is the type of oxygen that we breathe.

Once the oxygen molecules break off from their nitrogen molecules, the nitrogen molecules move along the surface of the catalyst looking to make friends with another nitrogen molecule. When it finds one, they bond and become the stable, harmless nitrogen in the atmosphere. After it becomes atmospheric nitrogen, its bond with the walls of the catalyst is weakened and the gas moves along to the second phase of the catalytic converter, oxidation.

When the gases have finished in the reduction stage of the catalytic converter, and all the nitrogen oxides have been eliminated, we are left with atmospheric nitrogen, atmospheric oxygen, carbon dioxide, carbon monoxide, water, and unburned fuel.

The oxidation stage of the catalytic converter uses platinum and palladium, which want to bond with the various oxides. The oxygen molecules bond with the surface of the catalyst and break up and eventually find carbon monoxide molecules to bond with, creating carbon dioxide. The carbon dioxide bond is stronger than the bond with the catalyst and moves through the matrix, allowing the process to begin again. While this is happening, some of the freed up oxygen molecules begin to bond with the unburned fuel (hydrocarbons) and are changed to water and more carbon dioxide.

This brief overview of the design of catalytic converters is important because it shows the advancements in cat technology. The original cats were very inefficient and clogged up quickly, causing serious performance issues. Modern performance catalytic converters are designed for free flow while doing their job of cleaning exhaust gases.

Magnaflow makes high-flow cats that meet the requirements of New York and the California Air Resources Board (CARB), such as the 53006 universal 2.5-inch unit. These cats ensure the emissions of your LS or LT swap matches the necessary specs for your area.

Air Intake

To maximize performance, an LS (and any other engine for that matter) needs a strong flow of dense air channeled into the engine. As you well know, when you pack more air into the combustion chamber, you pack in more fuel, and thus, you produce more power. Although mufflers and exhaust systems manage exhaust gases, the air intake determines flow into the engine and it must be tailored to the engine and application.

The 1969 Chevelle featured in this book uses a 90-degree elbow and a short section of tubing with a reducer to couple the MAF and air filter to the Holley throttle body. Creating your own kit with universal parts is an inexpensive way to get the job done. Locating the filter as close to the wheel well as possible yields the coolest air; the tubing length is not much of a factor as the run should be within a couple of feet of the engine in an A-Body.

Unlike the exhaust, the intake system is very simple; an air cleaner element, some tubing, and the MAF sensor are all that is required for the EFI LS and LT engine. It is possible on some swaps to simply install a cone-style air cleaner onto the throttle body with a built-in MAF sensor between them, but usually you need some sort of ductwork.

Large, smooth bends in the piping are the hallmark of an effective intake system; the air should not make abrupt turns. Sharp bends create a vortex effect inside the tube and can drastically slow the air. Slow air means less air in the engine. Short air filter elements require the air to make fast direction changes and that siphons off potential horsepower. The best bet is to make the intake tube as straight as possible, preferably grabbing the cooler air outside the engine bay.

This is not always possible, but most A-Bodies have plenty of room under the hood. For the Chevelle build in this book, a selection of components from Summit Racing and Spectre were used to match the 4-inch Holley throttle body to the 3.5-inch stock Vortec MAF sensor and cone-style air filter. A piece of 4-inch stainless steel tubing was installed between the 90-degree 4-inch silicone elbow for the throttle body. On the other side, a Spectre 4-inch to 3.5-inch stepdown was used to connect to the MAF sensor (I used a 1996 Camaro MAF) and then to the air filter.

Spectre produces vehicle-specific air intake kits for GM A-Body cars as well. These are year-specific and direct the airflow from the inner fender to the throttle body. Unlike universal systems and "piece-together" intakes, these feature smooth mandrel bends that reduce air turbulence and fit like they are factory.

Performance Project: Installing a Pypes Exhaust System

Swapping an LS engine is a lot of work. One of the most overlooked components of the job is the exhaust system. Often, it's overbuilt, producing less than superior performance. The most common mistake is running an exhaust that is simply too big for the engine. The exhaust piping is not solely intended to evacuate spent gases from the engine to the back of the car. In fact, the exhaust is an essential system that can create horsepower through scavenging, which in basic terms is the effect of pulling exhaust out of the engine by means of positive and negative pulses.

As each pulse of the engine pushes exhaust out, an opposite pulse pulls toward the engine. These pulses create a vacuum that draws additional gases out of the combustion chamber and can even draw fresh air/fuel into the chamber. The scavenging effect is directly related to the heat and tubing size. As the diameter of tubing increases, the pressure is reduced, dropping the temperature inside the pipe, which slows the gases, reducing scavenging.

On the opposite end of the spectrum, pipes that are too small restrict flow, produce high temperatures, and cause power loss. There is a compromise that yields the best for both flow and scavenging.

For a typical sub-500-hp street car, a 2½-inch exhaust is more than enough to support the flow of the engine while maintaining proper scavenging. As horsepower increases and surpasses the 500-hp mark, engines need a 3-inch exhaust to maintain proper flow.

These numbers are for mandrel-bent pipe, not for compression-style pipes as you source from most local muffler shops. Compression-bent pipes require larger diameters because the diameter changes drastically when bent.

Having the local muffler shop create and install a set of pipes gets the job done, but the cost of the system can far outweigh its benefits. Many local muffler shops are more interested in quantity than quality, so they use inferior products and tools. The welding can be poor, with large gaps between the pipes.

For a properly tuned exhaust, you need a system that was designed to fit your vehicle and perform as designed. Pypes Exhaust offers engineered systems for just about every vintage of muscle car available, as well as trucks, SUVs, and modern muscle applications. Each system is designed to produce efficient flow and properly fit the car. Pypes uses 409 stainless steel tubing for all its systems, ensuring a rust-free finish that lasts. For builders who want to take a step up, Pypes offers the 304 polished stainless kits.

Most Pypes systems come with a basic X-pipe, which balances the exhaust system. As an added option, you can upgrade to the X-Change X-pipe, which adds open-exhaust dumps after the X-pipe crossover. This not only gives you the ability to bypass the mufflers for racing, it also lets you keep the benefits of the X-pipe. Another unique feature of the X-Change X-pipe is that the exhaust dumps are straight out of the pipe, instead of on the curve, reducing the flow restriction when running the system open.

Pypes offers three levels of muffler performance: Street Pro, Race Pro, and The Violator. For the project Buick GS shown here, I chose Street Pro mufflers. These are great for cruising and not attracting local law enforcement, but still have a nice mellow rumble. If you prefer a more vocal exhaust, the Race Pro units are the way to go.

Installing the 2-1/2-inch 409 stainless system with Street Pro mufflers and an X-Change X-pipe on this 1971 Buick GS convertible was simple. The money you save on labor allows you to buy a better system. The pipes are slip fit, and can be installed using the included clamps. However, welding the exhaust is the best method, and the 409 stainless is easily welded with a standard MIG wire welder. The vehicle must be safely raised off the ground because this job requires working room under the car. Jack stands or ramps are a suitable replacement for a lift if you don't have access to one.

The first step is to lay the kit out on the floor. Look at the diagram. It is easy to place the parts the way you think they should go, but they might not fit that way. Make sure to test fit the pieces together because they don't always fit out of the box, and you don't want to fight it under the car.

With the old exhaust removed, install the new components. Start with the new hangers, then the rear pipes, going up and over the rear end. One person can do the job, but a second hand always helps. The mufflers should go on next, but it depends on the application and where the mufflers will be located.

Install the X-pipe assembly. This piece is important and comes unwelded. It should be centered under the driveshaft, and is directional; the arrow should point toward the engine, not the back of the car (it is a serious pain pulling it out and switching it around). Place the shorter front X-pipe tubes. These tubes may require trimming for the best fit, depending on the motor mounts and headers used.

The next step requires some fitting, measuring, cutting, and welding. Use a chop saw with a fresh blade, which costs only about $75. It makes things much cleaner and easier. Bolt or clamp the header collector reducers to the headers and slip on the tubes from the exhaust. With everything else in position, carefully measure the length of the tube. Mark the tube with a sharpie and pull the assembly from the car. Measure twice, if not three times. Cut off the excess tube and weld the tube to the reducer. Reinstall the assembly and make sure everything fits.

At this point, you can use clamps to hold the system together, but you should weld it for utmost strength and durability; the slip-fit design does not require welding the entire circumference of the pipes, which is nice, because it is a tight fit. A few well-placed tack welds suffice and ensure there are no leaks and that the pipes hold together. Standard MIG wire welds the 409 stainless tubing without issue, so get out your welder. Once that is done, the system is ready to fire up and enjoy.

1 With the Buick GS up on a set of Race Ramps (these really raise the car and are much safer than jack stands), there is enough room to work comfortably.

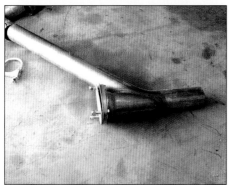

2 The Pypes kit's key feature is the optional X-change kit. It adds the well-designed dumps, sending the open exhaust straight out rather than making it turn as with most other dump pipe kits.

3 The Pypes exhaust is simple to install and includes all the hardware. I also opted for the polished stainless tips, which go on after the car is painted and the freshly chromed bumpers are installed.

4 Stainless steel mufflers feature slotted ends that facilitate the slip-on fit. I had to open these up a bit with a hammer to fit the pipes together. Don't worry; it was only a couple of taps. Once resized, I tapped the tabs to form fit the tubing.

5 The kit comes with a bunch of body clips and bolts to facilitate mounting the new hangers. They work on one side, but not the other. I placed the rear hanger just behind the gas tank on the frame.

6 Mount the muffler hanger on the rear crossmember in front of the rear end. These must go just like this or the pipes don't hang right.

7 The most difficult task is routing the over-axle tailpipes. The weight of the body needs to be taken off the suspension to gain the necessary clearance. Support the vehicle with jackstands and let the rear differential hang. Make sure you look at the diagram on the instructions; the pipes are side-specific. You don't want to have to do this twice.

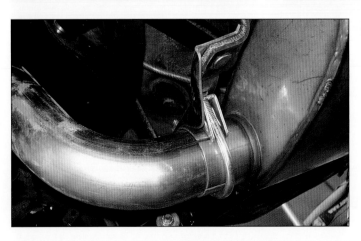

8 The mufflers install on the tailpipes in front of the rear end. The clamp mounts to the muffler, and then the remaining thread pushes through the hanger and the nuts go on. These need to be hand tightened only for now.

9 The X-pipe assembly is not welded together. It consists of three pipes: the X-Change pipe and two dump pipes. The rear section of the assembly links the dumps to the mufflers and to the X-pipe. The arrow on the X-pipe section must point toward the engine. These tubes may need to be trimmed for the best fit and to line up with the headers. The kit is designed to be clamped or welded together.

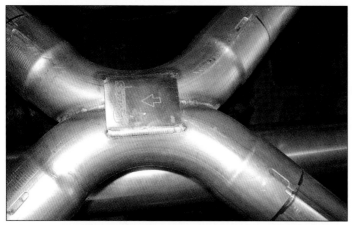

10 The X-pipe center section has an arrow that must point toward the front of the car. It is easy to mistake this as meaning the direction of flow. You really do need to read the instructions.

11 Remove any paint from the collectors (not shown) before welding.

12 Weld the collector pipes to the collector flanges using a MIG welder adjusted for 14-gauge steel.

13 With the collector reducers in place, mark the header-to–X-pipe tubing for length. This piece must be trimmed to fit, as different headers need different lengths pipe. If you are running manifolds or short headers, you need to order a downpipe for this section.

14 Using a Sharpie, mark the pipes for fitment. Measure three times, cut once. Your measurements vary based on transmission crossmember, headers, and a few other variables. Measurements for each swap project vary significantly.

15 I cut the pipe using a chop saw. Measure twice, cut once, because it is a lot harder to put it back on. Each side is likely different, so measure both sides.

16 The trimmed and welded header-to-pipe assembly completes the fitting stage. Bolt the reducer and torque it down before you begin welding. The kit includes clamps, and the exhaust system can certainly be clamped together long term. However, it is highly recommended that the system be welded together. Standard MIG wire easily welds the 409 stainless tubing.

17 The new exhaust system has been completed. The entire job should take one person about four hours. You can leave the mufflers clamped in place so that they can be removed a little easier if you choose to take them off.

Performance Project: How to Properly Dimple Headers

Headers help your engine breathe and efficiently manage exhaust gases, so your engine produces more power than stock exhaust manifolds. When installing headers in an A-Body swap project, interference issues often make fitting a set of headers difficult. Most aftermarket designs for the GM A-Body are well-tested, but some components don't always fit well together, so some adjustment is commonly needed.

Contrary to popular belief, dimpling headers makes no discernible difference in power. In fact, in some tests dimpling even increased power by a few ponies. One dyno test showed that even severe indentation of all eight primary tubes in multiple places had no adverse effect on performance. So now that you know it is okay and won't hurt your engine's performance, what is the best way to do it?

You have several methods for dimpling a header tube. Sometimes folks just go bananas with a hammer, but this leaves an ugly mess. Although you're able to resolve the clearance issue, it's not very scientific. Others suggest filling the tube with sand to add resistance; supposedly this makes a more uniform dent. The other method, the one I demonstrate here, uses heat to soften the steel, and a hammer to make the magic happen.

The first step to find the problem spot. On this Buick GS, I have a set of custom headers that were built to test the clearance of an LT1 in the A-Body. These are LS-swap headers with LT1 flanges. Unfortunately, the angle at the flange is not quite right, and the primary tubes hit the starter flange and the knock sensor on the passenger's side. Eventually, I will get a proper set of headers, but for now, dimpling is the answer.

Mark the headers with a sharpie at the interference points. Remove and load them into a sturdy bench-mounted vise. Then apply some heat with an oxy-acetylene torch in just the area you need to dimple. This is important, as you want to make just enough of a dent to clear the area, and you don't want to distort the surrounding pipe. Be careful not to melt through the tubing.

Once the pipe is glowing red, hit it with a ball-peen hammer in the center, working out. For smaller dimples, the round ball side is best, but for larger areas, use the flat side of the hammer. Then let the headers cool naturally. Placing them in front of a fan cools them in just a few minutes.

Check the fitment and perform any additional dimpling until the headers fit.

Although it is not something you want to do, it is often necessary to get the headers to clear the chassis or other engine components. Just be careful not to close the tube or cut a hole in it. If you do put a hole in it, you can always weld it up.

1 *Sometimes parts don't fit as they should, which is often true with headers. A 1-degree variance at the top of the head can be a couple of inches at the bottom. These headers were modified LS swaps with LT1 flanges. That didn't quite work as planned because the passenger's side hits the bellhousing. Sometimes there is not enough clearance with other underhood components. And sometimes these components cannot be repositioned, so the exhaust system needs to be dimpled.*

2 *Use a marker to designate the area of the exhaust that comes in contact with the bellhousing. These are the two pipes at issue, so they need to be dimpled.*

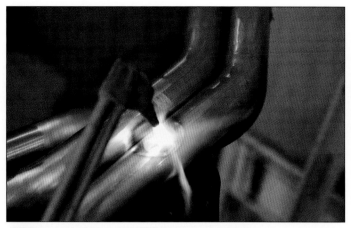

3 Using a torch, heat the pipe to cherry red. Be careful not to melt the metal. If the metal starts to spark, stop. Cherry red is all you need, work the torch in circles to expand the heated area as much as you need.

4 Hit the pipe with a hammer to dimple it. A ball-peen hammer is the best tool for this job; anything sharp could tear the tubing. This is a trial-and-error process and it usually takes a few tries to get it right.

5 This should get the job done on this pipe; next please.

6 Cherry red is the ticket to a smooth dimple. This allows for a more precise dent and not crushing the surrounding metal.

7 The ball side of the hammer is good for working the corners of the dimple. You want the dimple to be as smooth a transition as possible.